FRESNO'S WILSON ISLAND AND
ROSANNA COOPER WILSON, THE WOMAN BEHIND IT

FRESNO'S WILSON ISLAND AND

ROSANNA COOPER
WILSON

THE WOMAN BEHIND IT

JEANNINE RAYMOND, PhD

Rosanna Cooper Wilson, ca1893

Dear Georgie,

It has been moonlight and the silvery shimmer on the water was very beautiful. The old man in the moon high above is laughing at the romancing on the beach. He enjoys making them looney over each other . . .

Your mother has a little radio installed in the house. It is just fine and not much static. She gets many stations—The Fresno Bee, Los Angeles, San Francisco, San Jose, and Mexico . . .

> *With love and besos from your loving Grand-ma,*
> *Rosanna C. Wilson*

Written to her grandson, George Wilson Huffman (age twenty) from Santa Cruz, August 1, 1934

Palmetto Publishing Group
Charleston, SC

Fresno's Wilson Island and Rosanna Cooper Wilson, the Woman Behind It
Copyright © 2018 by Jeannine Raymond, Ph.D.
All rights reserved

First Edition

Printed in the United States

ISBN-13: 978-1-64111-240-6
ISBN-10: 1-64111-240-9

TABLE OF CONTENTS

Appendices:

FOREWORD

Rosanna Cooper Wilson is immediately relatable to me, if for no other reason, for her mixed-race heritage—a Mexican mother and father of English ancestry. Although I am not a native to California, I also spent a good portion of my childhood among family involved in the produce industry—specifically in an area known as The Valley in southern Texas, and specifically in the business of growing watermelons. I find Rosanna's story to be inspirational in its abundance of humanity, reality, and appreciation for the finer things in life.

Fresno's Wilson Island and Rosanna Cooper Wilson, the Woman Behind It is a story that originates in California family, politics, and power and results in turn-of-the-century Fresno opulence in residential architecture. It is a story that revolves around land, whether it be agriculture-related or solely in the context of real estate. It is a story of emotion and fact that contributes to the sense of place that not only surrounds us in Fresno but in central and northern California. This story transports readers to multinational destinations as well, which include the 1893 Chicago World's Columbian Exposition, a banana plantation in Mexico, and a European excursion before returning us home to Fresno.

The region of Fresno that includes what is now known as the Wilson Island Historic District is an architectural visualization of exclusivity designed for the "movers and shakers of the early 1900s in Fresno," which incorporated grand homes, the embodiment of various architectural styles, lush gardens, and immediate access to the streetcar system. Originally envisioned as a gateway to residential property, it also became a gateway to

Downtown Fresno as well as a character-defining anchor in the Tower District neighborhood.

Jeannine Raymond provides a comprehensive origin story of Fresno's Wilson Island Historic District and gives a voice to Rosanna Cooper Wilson's previously unwritten adventures and contributions. Upon reading *Fresno's Wilson Island*, one can't help but think of the famous words by Theodore Roosevelt: "Do what you can, with what you have, where you are." It is a lovely tribute to Rosanna and the centennial celebration for Wilson Island in 2019.

With warm regards,
Laura Groves van Onna
Historic Preservation Specialist
City of Fresno

PREFACE

What started twenty years ago as an effort to write the history of Fresno's Wilson Island Historic District—one of only four in the city—turned into a journey into the intriguing story of the woman behind it. It became more complex upon learning that she was a descendant of some of the most powerful and richest men in California in the 1800s—scions of Spanish concession and Mexican land grant families—and that she had been spurned as the eldest child of a marriage someone wanted to hide.

Her story demonstrates the connection between the established landowners of the vast ranchos in the fertile coastal valleys of Alta California in the 1800s and the involvement of their descendants in the development of land in California's Central San Joaquin Valley. Developing land was in Rosanna's genes. Taking risks was foundational to her success. Like her mother, she fell in love with an adventurer, though in Rosanna's case, it was someone who took her away from her home in Monterey County to bring her to Fresno in the middle of vast, uninhabited plains. The Wilson's North Fresno Tract, specifically the Wilson Island within it, is an example of how she turned her land into a catalyst for the northern expansion of residential Fresno in the late 1880s when the town was outgrowing its metropolitan center. Her personal oversight of construction in the Wilson Island ensured it would become a neighborhood for Fresno's elite at the turn of the twentieth century. Her diminutive stature belied her inner strength to achieve a vision consistent with contributions of her ancestors.

Current owners of the historic homes in the Wilson Island may enjoy learning about the original owners and getting a glimpse of how their neighborhood started, both the timing of its development and what led to the creation of a collection of museum-quality residences still well-maintained one hundred years later. The story takes a peek at life in Fresno in the early 1900s. Those interested in the achievements of a talented, strong woman overlooked by history may find the life of Rosanna Josefa Cooper Wilson and her connection to California's founding fathers as fascinating as I did.

The histories of the homes in the Wilson Island were the easiest to write. Hours of browsing through old books, public records, deeds and other original documents, and the abundance of online resources yielded volumes of information. It's much harder to unravel the life of someone born over 150 years ago—to get behind the veneer of a tough businesswoman and find the personal side of her that faded over the decades. The romantic who loved flowers and sang Spanish lullabies to her grandchildren. That requires reading between the lines, staring at photographs until the little details emerge, listening to stories she passed on to grandchildren. Listening beyond the words spoken. Her voluminous correspondence, original documents, and personal journal that her descendants graciously shared with me provided many insights. My hope is that this story accurately portrays the Rosanna that only exits now in the whispers of tales passed through the generations.

For those who would deny that she is descended from the Coopers and Vallejos, I can only offer that the facts have been carefully researched and documented. Her contributions to California's Central Valley continue the legacy of both families, something to be celebrated, not hidden. She was proud of her heritage and an example for women of all times of the importance of having the fortitude to push past immediate adversities while working toward a vision.

Among those who helped document her life events, at the top of my list, is Betsy Huffman Griffin, whose tendency to collect documents, photos, and correspondence (from three generations of prolific letter writers) has resulted in a treasure trove of information that has rightfully earned a spot in an archive somewhere in California. If it does end up in an archive, find a way to preserve the pressed flowers from her garden that are still in one of those 1893 letters! Without them, this story would have been a hollow reporting of facts.

Phil Long is a descendant of one of Rosanna's sisters. His hours of research spent collecting source documents and his mastery in organizing large amounts of information helped confirm critical relationships. But more than that, he was often a valuable sounding board throughout the tedious process of putting Rosanna's story together in alignment with the facts. We bumped into each other quite serendipitously when I ran across a random email posted on the web some twenty years ago when I first began sleuthing for information on Rosanna. It was a fluke find that sat in my files for the next two decades until I had the time to begin this project in earnest. His willingness to share documentation and photos relevant to Rosanna's story is much appreciated.

There are a number of people in roles that contribute to work like this. They are the archivists in historical societies and the Monterey Dioceses, the reference librarians in towns like Monterey and Castroville, and the librarians at the bigger archives like the Bancroft Library in Berkeley. They include the Fresno City and County Historical Society and the Fresno County Deputy Surveyor with an amazing knowledge of the people as well as the tract maps relevant to the Wilson Island. They are also the young docents at the missions whose enthusiasm for preserving the history of their respective charges is an encouraging reminder that there is another generation of people interested in the connection between the past and the present.

Perhaps most inspirational to this project was Rosanna's granddaughter and namesake, Rosanna Katherine Huffman, who I met decades ago when she was in her eighties. I cannot recall now how we met, only that her excitement about sharing her grandmother's story was infectious. Although my focus at the time was on the Wilson Island, it was clear that the story of its landowner was foundational to understanding the beginnings of this historic district. There was an urgency about Rosanna Katherine—a sense that if she didn't share what she knew first-hand about her grandmother, it would be lost forever. Although she has since passed, I owe her a post-humus debt of gratitude for taking the time to visit, occasionally pulling up at the house in her vintage Mercedes, to share yet another tidbit of information about the grandmother she clearly loved and the Wilson Island she created.

Acknowledgements

Where to begin. If I started at the beginning, I would exhaust the patience of the reader. In the interest of brevity yet accentuating the importance of collective efforts, I'll call out just a few to add to those mentioned elsewhere. At the very top of my list are William and KC, who each in his own way provides support, patience, and continual intellectual nourishment. And whose tendency to disappear into Dodger games for hours at a stretch gave me the time to escape to my writing.

Two Wilson Islanders passed on to me treasured volumes that made the work easier to do. Laird Durley, a former resident who, before moving away years ago, gave me his books and documents collected from other former residents so they could someday be used for the benefit of the Wilson Island. Barbara Jewitt, who passed on original volumes of the Vandor books with the same intent. Numerous people patiently read and edited drafts, graciously providing much-needed feedback. Among them is Jeanie Borba, another Wilson Islander, whose journalistic eye helped me see the real story in what I was struggling to assemble. And my longtime friend and colleague Tom Ebert, who supplied considerable editorial assistance in the early drafts and detailed information about Catholic practices which are somewhat of a mystery to me but an integral part of the story.

CHAPTER 1

THE EARLY YEARS, 1859 TO 1879
MONTEREY – SANTA CRUZ – CASTROVILLE

The secret alteration to Rosanna's original mission baptismal record:
"padre no conocido"

The story of the Wilson Island begins with Rosanna. Maria Rosanna Josefa Cooper Wilson was a petite woman of Mexican and English heritage who became a major contributor to the growth and development of the Central San Joaquin Valley town of Fresno, California, at the turn of the twentieth century. Her mother, Maria Eduvigues Soto, was a descendant of Spaniards who accompanied Father Junipero Serra to Alta California. Her father, John Baptist Henry Cooper (JBHC), was a descendant of an English father and a Spanish mother from a highly educated, influential family active in the Mexican Alta California government before it was acquired by the United States. Rosanna would spend much of her youth in the 1860s and 1870s on her father's land grant rancho, Bolsa del Portrero y Moro Cojo, near the coast of Monterey County and the fertile Pajaro and Salinas Valleys, and her adult years in Fresno, the agricultural hub of California's Central Valley.

She would overcome a fractured childhood, the cultural limits imposed on women of that era, the challenges of dealing with a mixed-race heritage and a domineering husband, and the bitterness of believing she had been tricked out of an inheritance she thought she was entitled to. Perhaps that caustic blow was the catalyst that transformed her into an astute businesswoman whose vision to expand Fresno's residential neighborhoods northward, shared by her husband, George, resulted in one of the city's historic treasures. She lived in an era where opportunities to influence the future of the state and to grow their wealth rewarded risk-taking investors, though women typically were not among them. It would take her five decades to overcome the hurdles put in her path by trusted family members, but, ultimately, she prevailed. Though she may not have benefited financially through inheritance to the degree she expected, she inherited something far more valuable than money . . . the tenacity and will to succeed, as well as a deep understanding of the long-term benefits of investing in land, a business of artful and cunning politics coupled with swift decision-making in the newly emerging state.

It was in this environment that Rosanna experienced heartbreaking loss in her childhood and youth. Separated from her mother and two of her sisters by the age of eleven, she lost her home, and subordinated her first language and roots. Rosanna was convinced by a grandmother that she was not worthy of the name she carried because of the perceived lower status of her mother's family despite decades as Alta California landowners. For much of her adult life, she sincerely believed she had been betrayed by her stepmother and half-brother, whom she accused of trying to deal her out of her rightful inheritance. From this crucible of chaos emerged a resilient, strong young woman who nonetheless in her later years would savor the memories of her childhood in the fertile coastal valleys as she listened to strains of "La Cucaracha." The challenges she encountered in her youth prepared Rosanna for those she would face later in life when she went on to create a legacy of historic significance for Fresno.

Rosanna's formative years were spent in the Pajaro and Salinas Valleys, more precisely in the arc around Monterey Bay defined by the cities of Santa Cruz to the north; Watsonville, Castroville, and Salinas in the middle; and ending in the south at Monterey. (See Appendix A, map of Monterey and Santa Cruz area.) Her early years straddled what are today the counties of Santa Cruz and Monterey, where notable Sotos and Borondas arrived in Alta California in the 1700s. Her maternal great-great-grandfather Ignacio de Soto was a member of the 1775 Anza expedition to Alta California and one of the first settlers of the city of San Francisco. Ignacio and Barbara Lugo de Soto received numerous ranchos through land grants. The nature of their business ventures is lost to history, but Rosanna remembered hearing stories of the Sotos dealing in imported goods from China.

Another maternal great-great-grandfather and patriarch of the Alta California Borondas, Josef Manuel Boronda, accompanied Father Serra on his second visit to Alta California. As a young soldier stationed at the Presidio in San Francisco, he began teaching. Following his marriage to Maria Gertrudes Higuera at the Mission Santa Clara de Assis in 1790, they gradually moved farther down the coast, ultimately settling in the Monterey area. The Borondas existed by subsistence farming and husbandry, bartering goods, and outside employment. They were respected in the Alta California community, and they often held minor governmental positions.[1]

Like the Sotos, they too benefited from land grants. Josef Manuel Boronda was granted The El Tucho Spanish Concession in 1795 as a retired Army soldier. The Borondas's 6,625-acre Rancho Los Laureles was in the upper Carmel Valley, which included today's Carmel Valley Village. The next generation of Borondas would acquire additional ranchos.

When Mexico won its independence from Spain in 1821, the Spanish practice of granting concessions to use government land changed under the new Mexican government to one of outright grants of land until 1848, when the United States acquired California. Land in early California was abundant. Spanish land concessions and Mexican grants to those who had a military or civil service record, as well as other private citizens, was strong incentive to populate the territory.[2] The Spanish—and later Mexican—governments were concerned about Russian fur traders encroaching on the Northern California coast beginning in the 1700s and hostile Indians from beyond the coastal mountain range and the Central San Joaquin Valley to the east. Establishing Spanish and Mexican families in the coastal regions was a strategic decision, along with creating the chain of presidios (military posts) and twenty-one Catholic missions along the coast. The Alcaldes—Mexico's highest-ranking administrators in Alta California in a role somewhat like a combination of judge and mayor—had the authority to grant land.[3] After the Mexican-American War ended in 1848, those who had land grants had two years to prove their ownership to the US government. Both Rosanna's maternal and paternal ancestors benefited from the concessions and land grant practices. The ranchos of these families were in some cases contiguous, particularly in the Salinas Valley area between today's Castroville and Carmel Valley.[4]

Rosanna's grandfather Juan Bautista Rogers Cooper, 1851

Up the road from the Sotos and next to the Borondas were the Coopers. The family patriarch was Rosanna's grandfather, John Rogers Cooper, a ship's captain born in Alderney, in the English Channel, in 1791, and raised in New England. In 1827, not long after Cooper arrived in Alta California, he converted to Catholicism, changed his name to the Spanish version, adopting the baptismal name Juan Bautista (John the Baptist) Rogers Cooper (JBRC), and married Geronima de Encarnacion Vallejo, younger sister of arguably the most powerful man in California at the time, General Mariano Guadalupe Vallejo.

Rosanna's grandmother Geronima de Encarnacion Vallejo Cooper

This marriage expanded JBRC's political connections and guaranteed his eligibility to acquire Mexican land grants. His lifetime land holdings were vast, but the two he held onto until he died extended from the coast (the two-Spanish-league, eight-thousand-acre El Sur Rancho) inland to Castroville near Salinas (Bolsa del Portrero y Moro Cojo). His first home, an adobe built in the center of the city of Monterey around the time of his marriage to Encarnacion, is today an historic site operated by the National Trust. (See Appendix B.)

JBRC was a well-known figure in California's business community throughout the 1800s. He never lost his love of the sea and continued well into his fifties sailing his ship, *The Rover*, between Monterey Bay, San Diego, China, Hawaii (then called the Sandwich Islands), and various ports in New Spain, later Mexico. Hawaii was a particularly important stop on the Pacific Rim route. It was not only an active port for vessels traversing the Pacific, but it was also the place where wealthy English-speaking Californians sent their children to attend missionary school. Spanish was the vernacular of Alta California, especially for business-men. But immigrant families from the East Coast wanted their children to retain fluency in English. Though his half-brother, Thomas Larkin, the first and only consul to the Mexican Alta California government, made desperate appeals to East Coast contacts to establish an English-language school in Alta California, it was not going to happen soon enough to sat-isfy JBRC's desire that his young son become fluent in English as early as possible. So JBRC ultimately sent his son and namesake to the Sandwich Islands to be educated in English by the missionaries, conveniently drop-ping him off en route across the Pacific.

In 1822, he sold his ship to the newly appointed Governor Luis Antonio Arguello (the first native-born governor of Alta California and the first under Mexican rule) and went into partnership with him in a lucrative sea otter hunting business that continued until 1841. Needing to find a new source of income by the 1850s, he engaged in smuggling goods from China and the Hawaiian Islands through landings on his El Sur Rancho, thus avoiding the high duties imposed at the Monterey port by regulations of the new US government. But somehow, he still needed to get the goods to Monterey for distribution to California markets. The solution was a cattle drive. He created the coast trail expressly for that purpose and imported Guernsey cattle from one of the Channel Islands to crossbreed stock. As a result, not only did he solve his smuggled goods distribution problem, but he developed the best breeding cattle in California. He initiated roundups and rodeos that lasted three days and attracted hundreds of people, including vaqueros from Monterey.

For decades, these events perpetuated the Spanish culture of the area, of which his son John Baptist Henry Cooper (JBHC) was very much a part. The "varsoviana," a dance brought to Alta California from Mexico, became the traditional dance at the El Sur Rancho rodeos. The son sent years earlier to the Sandwich Islands to be educated in English was a native Spanish speaker who also valued the Spanish culture of the rancho. JBHC, Rosanna's father, would ensure that the old Spanish traditions continued after his father's death. However, that legacy came to an end when JBHC's widow, Martha Cooper Hughes, sold the El Sur Rancho in 1928 (Wall, 1989).

The Cooper side of Rosanna's family included one more notable relative prominent in California history—her granduncle General Mariano Guadalupe Vallejo, whose sister married Rosanna's grandfather Juan Bautista Rogers Cooper. Geronima de Encarnacion Vallejo was a year younger than her famous brother, after whom the city of Vallejo in Solano County, California, is named.[5] He was the director of Mexico's colonization of the northern frontier and the founder of the city of Sonoma. He was also a member of the first Constitutional Convention of California, convened in October 1849 to draft the first state constitution. Among other things, he was assigned the task of describing the origin of the name of each of the new California counties because of his knowledge of Indian languages, English, Spanish, French, and Latin. He was arguably the wealthiest man in the state in that era.[6]

Rosanna's grand uncle, and her father's godfather General Mariano Vallejo

General Vallejo was also the godfather of Rosanna's father, JBHC, at his baptism in Cathedral San Carlos Borromeo in 1830 (also known as the Royal Presidio Chapel in Monterey). The Vallejos actively participated—personally and in business—in the Cooper side of Rosanna's family. Thus, Rosanna was the grandniece of a decorated general in the Mexican army deployed to maintain control of Alta California for the Mexican government. The man who has been referred to as the leader and spokesperson for the California-born, Spanish-speaking population of the 1800s, the man who made his case on land grantee rights to the Supreme Court and to President Lincoln himself. And he understood the importance of settling the northern frontier, even when it came to advocating for change under the American territorial acquisition (Vandor 1919, McKittrick 1944).

General Vallejo was a highly educated, gracious, and amiable man who was proud of being a pure-blood Spaniard and enjoyed the life of

a land baron in Sonoma, the town he created. He was comfortable testing the limits for higher causes, even if it meant challenging the church.
In his youth, he and two friends were temporarily excommunicated from
the Catholic Church for importing books by such authors as Voltaire,
Rousseau, and Telemachus, banned by the California clergy. The gallant
young men, eager to learn yet willing to make amends to the church, struck
a deal. In a clandestine effort orchestrated in the wee hours of the morning
at the San Francisco Presidio, he traded four hundred hides and ten kegs
of tallow (standard currency of that era) for what became the finest library
in California, kept in his home (McKittrick, 1944).

Encarnacion, his sister and Rosanna's grandmother, may not have been
as broadminded as her brother. She was very aware of the smuggling business her husband, JBRC, engaged in from the El Sur Rancho, though she
never visited the second home he built there for business trips. Although it
would have been easy from Monterey to take the ship to El Sur, she was too
susceptible to seasickness. Overland travel by rail or horse was beneath the
dignity of a woman of her age and status, so she remained at their home
in Monterey. Unfortunately, she took a dim view of her granddaughter
Rosanna for reasons that are the subject of family legend, something to do
with friction between the Sotos and Coopers (or Vallejos) over business dealings. Over the course of visits with Encarnacion, when Rosanna said she
occasionally "babysat" her grandmother, Encarnacion's alleged refusal to
speak to her granddaughter, or perhaps her occasional vitriolic comments,
made it clear to her impressionable young granddaughter that she did not
like the fact that Rosanna's mother was one of the Sotos, who, in her opin-
ion, were of a lower class than the Coopers or Vallejos. The feeling of being
second-rate, especially in her grandmother's eyes, had a searing, devastating
impact on the young girl that would remain with her forever, passed on years
later in conversations with her own granddaughter.

In addition to JBRC's extensive cattle ranching and trading activity
of the 1800s (in hides, tallow, sea otter pelts, and general merchandise),

his ranching investments included lucrative wheat and barley cash crops grown in the Pajaro Valley. In 1828, JBRC rented Rancho Bolsa del Pajaro from Sebastian Rodriguez to build a grist mill, house, corrals, and barns (Koch, 1973). It also generated profits in hides and tallow before he turned it back over to Rodriguez in 1832, the year before he was granted the El Molino Rancho, one of his first land acquisitions. Almost eighteen thousand acres were granted to him by the governor in 1833, extending south from the Russian River along Atascadero Creek and encompassing present-day Forestville. Its name refers to Cooper's sawmill, the first to be built in California.[7]

JBRC had six children, but the only son to produce heirs was John Baptist Henry Cooper (JBHC), Rosanna's father, who, like his father before him, fell in love with a woman descended from Spanish land grant families. As the story goes, in 1857, twenty-nine-year-old JBHC eloped with his eighteen-year-old Alisal neighbor, Maria Eduvigues Soto, daughter of Andres Soto and Josefa Escolastica Espinosa.[8]

Eduvigues Soto holding her first daughter Rosanna , ca 1860

Rosanna's father John Baptist Henry Cooper

John was often in Castroville on family business and had owned land in neighboring Alisal since at least 1851. Towns then were sparsely populated, and travel between them and the ranchos was often by horseback. It is not inconceivable that he first met Eduvigues when business called him to the Alisal area. Legend has it that they left secretly on horseback one night headed for Daly City, where they were married in a civil ceremony. Whether a civil union or a common-law marriage, it would last less than a decade. If there was a marriage in the church, no record of it has ever surfaced. The Catholic Church required the publication of marriage bans for weeks prior to any nuptial ceremony and would not have permitted JBHC to remarry later in 1871 without some evidence that his relationship with Eduvigues either ended in a civil divorce, for which there is no record, or that there had never been any wedding ceremony at all in the eyes of the church.

Rosanna was their first child, born on December 7, 1859, in Alisal, also referred to today as East Salinas, a short distance from Castroville.[9] The closest post office was in Natividad, which also hosted a bustling stage coach station in the 1850s until traffic was rerouted to Salinas. Baptizing her daughter in not only a Catholic church, but at the chapel in Monterey where generations of her husband's and her own family members had been baptized, was important to Eduvigues. Thus, when Rosanna was five months old, they journeyed to Monterey to have her baptized at the Royal Presidio Chapel, San Carlos Borromeo Cathedral on May 5, 1860, a ceremony typically attended by generations of the families of both parents. She was the first child of the scion of one of California's wealthiest families at that time, and one of the first grandchildren of Juan Bautista Rogers Cooper and his wife, Geronima de Encarnacion Vallejo Cooper.

*Royal Presidio Chapel, Monterey (San Carlos Borromeo Cathedral) where
Rosanna and previous generations of her family were baptized.*

12

Altar in the Royal Presidio Chapel much as it looked when Rosanna was baptized here in 1860.

Over the next six years, three more daughters were born to John and Eduvigues. In a family where land was the common currency, if her father were going to give her mother anything of value, it would be land. Thus, in 1867, when Rosanna was seven and a half years old, her father gave Eduvigues land in Alisal near the Salinas River, a combination of the property he had owned since 1851 and an additional adjacent newly purchased twelve acres. By then, Eduvigues was living in Castroville with their four daughters: Rosanna, Delfina (born in 1862), Guadalupe (born in 1864), and Francisca (born in 1866). Their father appears to have been setting them up with either a home or income as his business activities and attention shifted north to Monterey. But the hub of state business was gradually moving from Monterey further north to San Francisco. If John was to remain at the center of California commerce as well as ranching, he would have to join the migration without losing a foothold in the Monterey area. Within three years, he would move into his father's new house in San Francisco, leaving Eduvigues and the girls behind with the bit of land he gave them.

Eduvigues may have moved to Castroville after the birth of Rosanna in Alisal to be closer to the Sotos and Borondas, who were living there at the time, or simply to move into a bigger town. The young, first-time mother needed the support of her family. From the beginning, her husband was often away. As the eldest son in a family of growing power and influence in the state, JBHC was heavily involved in the family business and had been since the age of at least eighteen. From a relatively young age, he was accustomed to carrying substantial responsibility and wielding authority. With the birth of each of their daughters, Eduvigues carried on at least one of their family traditions by traveling to Monterey with her parents, who served as godparents, so the girls could be baptized in the Royal Presidio Chapel like generations of Cooper and Soto family members before them.

As the years passed, the relationship between Eduvigues and JBHC began to fray at the edges, thrusting Rosanna at age eleven into a situation that changed the course of her life. The specifics are murky, the details lost to generations of discord and conflicting accounts. But one thing is clear—by 1870, the family such as it was had disintegrated. Rosanna's whereabouts at that time are uncertain, but she was not in Alisal, nor was she with her mother and other sisters in Castroville. Her father had left them to relocate to San Francisco, where he took up residence with his parents and siblings in their relatively new home at 821 Bush Street.[10] Earlier, John's father (JBRC) had moved the family north when he decided their future was in San Francisco, not Monterey. However, they did retain a home on their ranch near Castroville. John became the workhorse of the family's second generation, overseeing work at El Sur and at the Bolsa del Potrero ranch in the Salinas-Castroville area near where Eduvigues and his daughters lived.[11]

Given the fact that the church did not recognize the validity of JBHC's common-law relationship with Eduvigues, the situation was always fraught with the possibility of dissolution. Her father's move to San Francisco signaled the end of a relationship that JBHC could walk away from. Another woman had come into her father's life. After setting Eduvigues up with land in Alisal, and following his subsequent departure to San Francisco, JBHC, now forty years old, remarried in 1871 in a church ceremony at Cathedral San Carlos Borromeo in Monterey to the eighteen-year-old Martha May Brawley, also from Monterey, twenty-two years his junior and reportedly a very strong-willed woman. In fact, it was rumored at the time that Martha had coerced JBHC into marriage with a claim of being pregnant (though no child materialized, at that time anyway). Martha's father was one of Cooper's tenant farmers near his sprawling Castroville Moro Cojo ranch.

Martha Brawley as a young woman, and as the "grande dame of Monterey Society."
Monterey State Historic Park Association newsletter, July-September 2014.

Immediately after their marriage, JBHC built the house in Castroville at Speegle and Merritt Streets (considered one of grandest in Monterey County) and made this his headquarters.[12] Feeling obligated in some way to his common-law daughters, upon his marriage to Martha, he brought Rosanna and eventually Delfina to this home to begin the next chapter in their lives with him and their stepmother. Why he only wanted Rosanna at first remains a mystery, along with the reasons for leaving the youngest two behind with their mother.

*The Cooper house in Castroville that JBRC built for Martha,
ca 1871. Corner of Speegle and Merritt Streets*

The Cooper house in Castroville as it looked in 2016. As of 2018 it is no longer visible from the street.

The initial stress of being separated from their mother's arms and the companionship of their siblings had occurred several years earlier. Rosanna had been sent to the convent boarding school in Santa Cruz near the Holy Cross Church to learn English at the age of seven, followed later by Delfina. They never lost their native Spanish, like their parents and grandparents before them. When Rosanna's father did come to visit them at school in Santa Cruz, these were joyful occasions. She recalled that he would occasionally bring a woman she did not recognize, perhaps her soon-to-be stepmother, Martha.

By the time Rosanna was about eleven, her parents separated, and her father remarried. It is not clear why her father brought only Rosanna to his new home in Castroville near his ranch and into the care of a woman, only seven years older, for whom Rosanna was a daily reminder of her husband's first love. Rosanna was lonely and depressed without her sisters. She cried incessantly in particular for her sister Delfina Eduvigues until her father finally gave in and retrieved Delfina as well. The two oldest daughters lived in the Cooper house for the next eight years, with the possible exception of the times they may have been at the boarding school in Santa Cruz. During those eight years, the family expanded as Rosanna and Delfina acquired four half-siblings: Alicia (1872), John BRC, Jr. (1873), Abelardo (1876), and Alfred Henry (1880).

Rosanna Cooper at age 16.   *Delfina Cooper at age 14.*

Though it is impossible to know how she felt at the time beyond the sadness and confusion of a young child whose world has been upturned, one wonders how a child of eleven explained to herself why her mother and two sisters had been left behind when she and Delfina were moved to their father's ranch. It is not known what her father may have told her on his occasional visits with them at school or what explanations her stepmother might have provided. We can only imagine how her mother tearfully said goodbye in an undoubtedly traumatic scene for both mother and daughter. There is no evidence they ever met again, though they may have exchanged glances if they occasionally passed each other on the streets of Castroville, where they all lived. Nor did Rosanna leave any writings that might provide us with insights into how she coped with the separation from her birth mother, or what she thought at the time about her young stepmother, young enough to be a sister, or the arrival of half-siblings. The one constant source of strength throughout her life was Delfina, who remained with Rosanna her entire life. Delfina's gravestone provides a hint of the importance they placed on recognizing both of their birth parents: "Daughter of I. Soto and JBH Cooper." Ida Soto[13] and John Baptist Henry Cooper.

Their new home was the stately Cooper residence at the corner of Speegle and Merritt Streets in downtown Castroville (still there today), which her father had built for his new wife, Martha. In the eyes of a child, it was huge, cavernous, a playground of secret spaces and endless rooms and hallways. Those rooms would soon be filled with the bustling arrival of four half-siblings (Merritt, 1881). In the meantime, Rosanna was becoming the eligible young daughter of one of the richest men in the county, if not the state. So it is not surprising that in 1879 she should catch the eye of the suave, ambitious son of a well-known Santa Cruz miller/farmer turned businessman, George Albert Wilson, who proposed to her.

Rosanna Cooper, about age 19.

George Albert Wilson, about age 23, possibly around the time of his marriage to Rosanna.

Born on February 1, 1856, George was average height at five foot eight and a half inches, of fair complexion, with gray eyes and light, naturally curly hair. His parents were among the many immigrants to California from the east—his father, Oscar Paulette Wilson, from New Jersey; and his mother, Lydia A., from Illinois. When he was a small boy, George's parents had moved the family to Santa Cruz, where he spent most of his youth. He had many relatives around Illinois and Wisconsin and at least one cousin in Seattle with whom he stayed in contact. But it would not be until 1893 when he went to Chicago to manage the Fresno exhibit at the World's Columbian Exposition that he would have an opportunity to meet any of them.

He was an adventurer who, at the age of twenty, set out from the Salinas Valley on a journey that included Los Angeles and Arizona. Exactly where he went and why is something he never talked about, nor did he leave notes for later generations to discover and ponder. The odyssey was the beginning of a lifetime of exploring opportunities beyond what was immediately visible. When he finally returned to Santa Cruz three or four years later, he engaged in the warehouse business (Davis 1915). He could not have predicted at the time how this work would benefit him in the future. It was through this job he learned the ropes in an industry that was foundational to at least two of his future business ventures—wheat and bananas.

By this time, Rosanna had matured into a diminutive, dark-haired, brown-eyed young woman who had inherited the "Cooper nose" along with their cachet. Marrying the nineteen-year-old eldest daughter of the power elite would have been a step up for twenty-four-year-old George. His bride-to-be was also a descendant of generations of Catholic ancestors. George was not Catholic, nor was he baptized into that church. In fact, George was a Freemason like his father, Oscar. Special dispensation from the bishop permitted the marriage on October 15, 1879, at Our Lady of Refuge Church in Castroville, where George's father, Oscar, and his sister, Milificent, served as witnesses.

Our Lady of Refuge Church, Castroville, California. ca 1930 (courtesy of the Monterey Diocese Archives)

Altar in Our Lady of Refuge Church where Rosanna Cooper and George Wilson were married in 1879. (courtesy of the Monterey Diocese Archives)

Our Lady of Refuge Church, Castroville, California. 2018

"Mr. and Mrs. J. B. H. Cooper request the pleasure of your company at the marriage of their daughter, Rosanna, to G. A. Wilson, on Wednesday, October 15, 1879, at 9 o'clock, P.M., at their residence, Castroville, Cal."

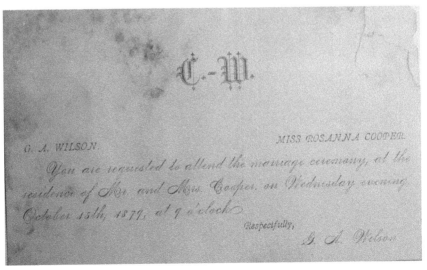

Invitation sent by the groom: "You are requested to attend the marriage ceremony at the residence of Mr. and Mrs. Cooper on Wednesday evening, October 15th, 1879, at 9 o'clock. Respectfully, G. A. Wilson."

Rosanna's father and stepmother expressed their affection for their daughter in their announcement of her wedding and in hosting the large gala nuptial event that included a sumptuous midnight supper at their mansion—considered one of the grandest in Monterey County—but a few blocks from Our Lady of Refuge Church. Presumably to ensure the Wilsons were adequately represented, in addition to the Cooper wedding invitations, George sent his own invitations. Guests traveled several hours from up and down the Pajaro and Salinas Valleys—from Santa Cruz, Watsonville, Salinas, Monterey, and Santa Rita—to attend one of the biggest social events of the season. The evening procession along the two blocks from the church to the Cooper's home must have been a spectacular display of Spanish finery. Delfina, her sister's bridesmaid, sang a duet followed by an instrumental duet played with Rosanna for their guests. Sadly, in the lengthy description captured in the Salinas newspaper at the time, there is no mention of Rosanna's mother or her other two sisters. If her mother came—it's doubtful she attended—the Salinas reporter overlooked her presence to focus on more prominent attendees. The chasm between Rosanna and the Soto side of her life had grown. And JBHC's past relationship was quietly papered over.

Left to right, front seated: Rosanna, Delfina, Martha in white. Left to right standing in back: George, three unidentified friends.

24

The newlyweds moved into a place provided by Rosanna's father on his ranch in Monterey County, at or near Cooper Switch, south of Castroville on the Pajaro Valley Consolidated Railroad (PVCRR) line and not far from the Cooper family home at Speegle and Merritt Streets in Castroville. It's not clear why that location was selected for the newlyweds. Availability of a house at an important location on the Cooper ranch? Proximity to the Cooper house in Castroville? Or to George's wheat venture? Cooper Switch was clearly a hub of agricultural activity. By August 1882, a Western Union line had been added, suggesting it was a key stop on the railroad that supported Spreckels beet sugar production. (See Appendix C, map of PVCRR showing Castroville and Cooper Switch.) Whatever the reason, Rosanna's father had provided well for his eldest daughter because with the house, of course, came land. It was a comfortable place to start a family, and soon, children arrived: first, their son, Albert Paulette (AP), on October 11, 1880, followed by their daughter, Lorena Rose, on September 12, 1884. Delfina remained nearby with her father and stepmother.

Albert Paulette Wilson (AP), about one year old.   *AP, about three years old.*

George was now a member of one of the valley's most prestigious families, and he knew he needed to upgrade his written communication skills and penmanship, especially in an era when formal and business communications were handwritten. He did not wait long to invest in a self-help manual. In December 1881, he purchased *Hill's Manual of Social and Business Forms: A Guide to Correct Writing*. In addition to lessons on proper cursive writing, it included guidance on everything from general laws of etiquette to wedding invitations, parties, and ceremonies. He practiced quietly at home while continuing to work as a miller and farmer, like his father, Oscar. However, within a few years, he would become an investor and developer, also like his father. His first move was a joint investment in wheat storage with Rosanna's uncle, Eusebius Joseph Molera, a graduate of the Royal Academy of Engineering in Madrid, Spain.

The Hills Manual of Social and Business Forms: a Guide to Correct Writing which George used to practice his handwriting and letter writing.

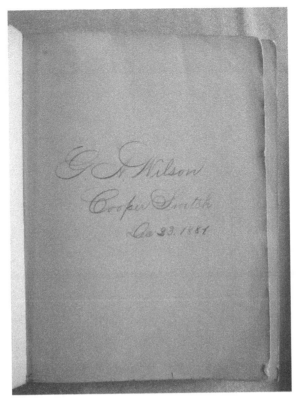

George's signature inside the manual: G. A. Wilson, Cooper Switch, Dec 23, 1881

Rosanna was George's connection to an extensive business community that is best understood by reflecting on her impressive heritage and the circumstances preceding the move to her father's home in Castroville. It also may shed some light on why she found this adventurer from Santa Cruz so appealing. She had grown up at the confluence of four established Alta California families in the Santa Cruz and Monterey County area who knew each other well. They represented five generations from Spanish and Mexican roots (the Sotos, Borondas, and Vallejos) and the Coopers, with English roots via New England, who collectively forged early business ventures and built ranching and commercial empires in Alta California. Rosanna may have seen her marriage to George as a means to escape the twists and turns of family relationships which she could neither understand nor control.

John did something interesting in 1872 after the birth of his first child with Martha, Alicia. Perhaps he was beginning to think of setting up inheritances for his children. One can only speculate as to why he gave land to Rosanna and Delfina, who were only thirteen and ten, respectively. Interestingly, the city agent at the time went to the trouble of confirming in writing that Martha agreed to the transaction and would not attempt to change it in the future. They each received large lots that began one street away from their home at the corner of Merritt and Speegle Streets in Castroville and extended down to the Tembladera Slough. Little did their father know it was not the only land each of his daughters would own. With that gesture, he lit an ember that would glow for generations.

While life for Rosanna and Delfina remained secure within the confines of the Cooper ranch, outside, their two younger sisters, Guadalupe and Francisca, were still living with Eduvigues somewhere in Castroville. There may have been numerous reasons for leaving the two youngest behind with their mother while their father first brought Rosanna and then Delfina to his new home on Merritt Street. Maybe the two youngest girls still needed their birth mother. They were only six and four at the time of their parents' separation. Perhaps four young girls would have been too much for his eighteen-year-old new bride to handle, especially having become pregnant with their first child several months later in about September 1871. Baptismal, confirmation, and census records provide some clues as to the relationship between Eduvigues and JBHC, which appears to have been compromised by the time Guadalupe was born in 1862. Whereas Juan Cooper and Eduvigues Soto were recorded in the baptisms at the Cathedral of San Carlos Borromeo as the parents for both Rosanna and Delfina, Guadalupe's record is different. There is no father's name, simply "N.N." (unnamed), and Francisca's confirmation record states the parents are Juan (i.e., John) and Eduvigues Soto. It is impossible to determine now if "Juan Soto" was an error or another effort to hide Juan Cooper's identity, this time in a different way. The baptismal records provide another clue supporting the assumption that theirs was a common-law marriage.

At the time, Catholic baptismal records distinguished between "legitimate children," born to parents who married in the church, and "natural children," born of parents unmarried in the eyes of the church. In each case where the father's name is listed, the girls are referred to as the natural daughter of Juan and Eduvigues. Finally, though Eduvigues may not have wanted to mention Juan Cooper's name as Guadalupe's father to the priest at the time of her baptism, she did not hesitate to tell the census enumerator eight years later in 1870 that her daughter's surname was Cooper. With the passage of time, problems sometimes dissipate. The perceived need for alterations made to the records in the early 1870s to hide JBHC's identity as the father of his four daughters was no longer of concern a few years later. By the time Rosanna and Guadalupe married in the Our Lady of Refuge Church in Castroville, their marriage records clearly state once again that JBHC is their father. Perhaps the records at the Castroville church were of little interest to nuptials at the cathedral in Monterey where JBHC married Martha May Brawley in March 1871.

John Long and Gaudalupe Cooper around the time of their marriage, 1882

Missions were the hub of family life events and the place where baptisms and marriages were formally recorded. Members of Rosanna's family were christened and married at the Cathedral San Carlos Borromeo in Monterey, at the Mission Santa Clara, and at the Mission San Miguel. Rosanna and her mother, Eduvigues Soto, were baptized at Cathedral San Carlos Borromeo (known today also as the Royal Presidio Chapel). Rosanna's grandparents were married in that mission. In fact, Cathedral San Carlos Borromeo[14] was the center of family baptisms and marriages for generations of Sotos, Borondas, and Coopers—all established Alta Californians.

As sacred as the mission records are, they are not impervious to malicious intentions. Unbeknownst to Rosanna, most likely around 1870, someone tampered with the records pertaining to her birth. Mission records are important confirmation of her heritage. Before the 1880s, states did not issue birth, marriage, or death certificates. Therefore, other records were used to determine familial relationships. Foremost among them were the Catholic baptismal records used by courts to establish lineage. Marriage records were not pertinent to determining parentage since they were not recorded contemporaneously with the birth. Only the baptismal record mattered. Therefore, the accuracy of church baptismal records was of critical importance. Any attempt to alter them or change the official record for less than honorable purposes would have devastating consequences for the person targeted. Decades later, Rosanna would learn of a deceitful attempt to redact her father's name from her baptismal record in an effort to hide her relationship to the Coopers. The rippling impact would be felt by generations of her descendants.

The mystery surrounding how Rosanna's baptismal record was altered and why is unresolved. The priest's robe rustled as he carefully opened the book of baptismal records to the page with Rosanna's entry, dipped the quill pen in heavy black ink, and secretly scratched out her father's name, John (Juan) Bautista Cooper, to write above it "padre no conocido" (father unknown), then went on to scratch out the Cooper family name in the margin. Sometime later, another priest drew a line down to the bottom of that page where he signed a statement confirming he saw the original entry with the true name of her father as John (Juan) Cooper. The susurrus of the robes of the first priest scratching his pen repeatedly across the page reverberated for generations, and the pain inflicted by the surreptitious deed was as sharp as the point of that quill pen, though not discovered until years later. The action was also an indication of the discontent, perhaps disdain, that someone in the family had for JBHC's daughters by Eduvigues and the lengths that individual would go to in an effort to obliterate the existent of his first family.

After she and John separated, Eduvigues remained in Castroville, where she married Charles H. Bambach, a local musician, in March 1876. She lived the rest of her life in Castroville, where her children by both JBHC and Bambach were married at the Our Lady of Refuge Church. Her love for Rosanna never waned, poignantly revealed in her funeral announcement years later after her death in 1901 in Colma, near San Francisco. Maybe it was news of her first love's passing just two years earlier that renewed a desire to reach out to their eldest daughter. Whatever the reason, of her two surviving daughters by JBHC, only Rosanna is specifically mentioned in the invitation to attend her mother's funeral. It is not known if Rosanna attended the funeral in Colma or if she communicated with her mother throughout their lives. If she remained in contact with Eduvigues; her two sisters, Guadalupe and Francisca (both of whom died at young ages); or the Soto and Boronda sides of her family, she made no mention of it to her children, nor did she mention them in any correspondence saved over the years. As an adult, Rosanna preferred to be known simply as Rosanna Cooper Wilson.

This is the family George had married into. He undoubtedly knew of the numerous family businesses, legacies of generations of landowners. Their land holdings were public, tangible, visible, and extensive. It's unlikely he knew of, or was even marginally aware of, the complexities resulting from broken relationships, altered church records, or the depth of resentment and jealousies between family members. Even if Rosanna did not explain her situation, Castroville was (and still is) small enough that he must have known about his father-in-law's common-law marriage with Eduvigues. They all attended the same church where the girls from that marriage were married. They all walked down the same main street, and though accidental encounters were possible, we will never know for sure if or when such meetings may have occurred. Perhaps given that Rosanna and George's home was outside of Castroville on the Cooper Ranch, her new circumstances were the beginning of a healthy separation from her past and an opportunity to grow. As she turned twenty in December 1879, a new bride in a new home on her father's ranch, Rosanna was beginning to focus on life with someone who would soon take her away from the familiarity of life in Castroville and the scenes of a painful past to embark on an adventure that would open doors she never dreamed of. Sadly, George would not live long enough to learn of the clandestine actions in the mission records and their impact on Rosanna. That revelation she would experience alone.

CHAPTER 2

ADVENTURE AND GROWTH,
1886 TO 1911

George's father, Oscar, may have been the only member of his family to venture out to California from Illinois, where he presumably met his wife, Lydia. They settled in Gilroy, where they started a family with the birth of George followed by two brothers—Frank B. (born in 1858) and Oscar, Jr. (born in 1867)—and one sister, Mary E. ("Mellie" or "Melificent," born in 1861). The senior Oscar had been a well-known, experienced miller for a number of years in Santa Cruz before becoming involved in a mining enterprise in that area. However, it was his milling expertise that would bring him to Fresno's attention.

George's father, Oscar Paulette Wilson   *George's youngest brother, Oscar Wilson, Junior*

George Albert Wilson

Over a period of six years, father and sons were part of the wave of eager entrepreneurs and skilled craftsmen seeking to profit from the growth of California's Central Valley. Each one of them had different interests and talents to invest. George's brother Frank led their migration to Fresno, followed by their father, then Oscar, Jr., and finally George with his new family. Frank arrived in Fresno in 1880 at the age of twenty-two, when the Fresno County population was less than ten thousand. The town had sprung up only eight years earlier as a stop on the railroad. Frank's position as a clerk in the Fresno store of general merchants Sachs and Henghi provided opportunities to participate in the talk in the business community about petitioning the state to incorporate the City of Fresno. The discussion had been going on for at least the last three years, well before he arrived, and it would continue for another five years before any action would be taken. Frank could see that Fresno lacked the infrastructure to support increased growth, so when the opportunity arose in July 1885 to sign a petition to incorporate, he added his signature to those of 120 other Fresno businessmen.

Fresno in 1886 from the back of the courthouse. Vandor 1919

Within a year of Frank's arrival in Fresno, their father, Oscar, was motivated to relocate to the Central Valley following his unsuccessful investment in a mining company in Santa Cruz. Oscar had been well known in
the Santa Cruz area and owned several parcels of land including one that
was part of the Coralitos Ranch. Beginning in 1868, he sold several of his
properties, notably 193 acres in Pajaro Township (for $900, or $15,200 in
2018) to the Santa Cruz Coal Mining Company. By 1873, he was a major
shareholder in that mining company.

However, the mining business soon soured. By the end of 1873
and through the next spring, a large number of his mining shares
were sold at public auction to cover the cost of delinquent assess-
ments. Lawsuits followed. And soon, Oscar renewed his interest in
milling—if he ever lost it in the first place—and turned his attention
to a start-up flour mill in Santa Cruz. In 1879, he was appointed to
the Committee on Plans and Specifications. His expertise in building and operating flour mills gained him a reputation that extended beyond Santa Cruz. So, it was no surprise to find him in Fresno
the following year, where he embarked on building a similar mill. In
mid-1880, he was off to San Francisco to procure special-order machinery for the Fresno mill, and by February of the following year,
he had a work crew busy with construction. The large grist mill was
located just east of the new St. John's Catholic Church downtown
around Mariposa and R Streets. A contract with the Fresno Canal
and Irrigation Company secured the water necessary to run the mill
capable of delivering an estimated three hundred barrels a day, equal
to any mill in the San Joaquin Valley.

The town had confidence in Oscar's experience running grist mills
and considered the completion of this one an indication of the healthy
growth of Fresno and its ability to support a larger population. "One by
one the solid enterprises are coming, and our town continues to boom"

(*Fresno Morning Republican* 1880). Interest in the mill was intense as the newspaper reported monthly on construction progress from November 1880 until it opened in June 1881. Within a year, the Champion Mills was producing the best cracked wheat ever seen using superior quality wheat and the latest improved machinery.

Oscar's confidence in his ability to deliver the mill was bolstered by his eagerness to join his son Frank in Fresno. With the machinery ordered, the water contract in place, and construction fully underway, he left his home in Redwood City, heading permanently for Fresno in May 1881, at the age of fifty-five. He was part of that wave of skilled professionals who saw Fresno's growth as guaranteed income for creative minds and willing workers. A later example of how he put his mechanical expertise to work is the pumice press he invented, which was tested in April 1890 at a local vineyard. So efficient at extruding the juice from grapes, it was touted by winemaker Hillstrom as the wine press of the future.

Frank and Oscar undoubtedly shared their enthusiasm with George, who was back in Castroville looking for an opportunity to recover from a failed business venture. He and Rosanna's uncle Eusebius J. Molera were in the grain silo and shipping business together near Cooper Switch on the Pajaro Valley Consolidated Railroad. Wheat crop failures due to a drought impacted their business, and attempts to seek help from his father-in-law, JBHC, were unsuccessful. JBHC was not going to invest in anything to do with wheat in the middle of a drought. It was time to move on. George's purchase of a horse in September 1886 for $100 from the neighboring Boronda family, close relatives of Rosanna, was either part of the preparations for the move to Fresno (a two-day journey from Castroville by horse and wagon) or a continuing investment in the land on the Cooper's Bolsa del Portrero y Moro Cojo Rancho.

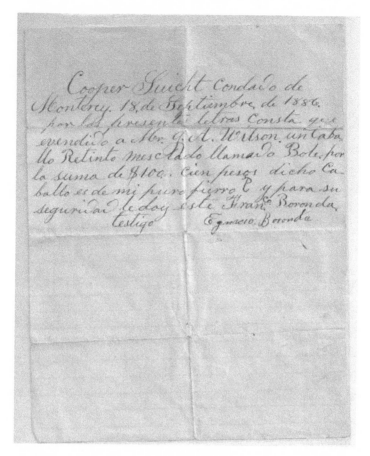

Bill of sale for a shiny black horse purchased by George Wilson for the sum of $100 from Franco Boronda and carrying his brand. Cooper Switch, September 18, 1886.

So it was in 1886, after seven years of trying to make a go of it living on the Cooper ranch, George enthusiastically gathered up Rosanna, their two young children (ages six and two), and his sister-in-law Delfina, left their home in Castroville and Rosanna's family, and joined those immigrating to Fresno during its biggest population boom to date. Founded by the Central Pacific Railroad Company in 1872, in 1886, Fresno was uninviting at best, with barren sand plains in all directions.[15] He may have had many reasons to uproot his family and head to California's

Central Valley. The failure of his wheat silo and shipping business due to a drought, his brother's and father's presence in Fresno, the opportunity to separate himself and his family from the complex web of familial and business relationships that defined his wife's family, or the fact that Fresno's incorporation the year before in 1885 opened the door for rapid expansion and entrepreneurial opportunities. Perhaps all of them, but for certain the latter.

In any case, for Rosanna, it was the second separation in her young life. Whereas George had seen the world outside of California, she had never been outside of the fertile coastal valleys where she had grown up. She left behind her family—her roots—for an unfamiliar destination two days' journey away. A place from which anyone with the means to do so escaped the brutal summer heat by going up into the foothills or over to the coast. Eventually, Rosanna would return to Santa Cruz to build a summer cottage, but that was a long way off. In the meantime, the young mother of two children remained connected to the Cooper family on Rancho Bolsa del Portrero y Moro Cojo in Castroville as best she could by exchanging letters with her father until his death in 1899.[16]

Likewise, George never completely severed his ties to the coast. Ever on the hunt for land, in later years he would pursue buying one thousand acres from the David Jacks Corporation on the southeast side of the county road about six or seven miles from Monterey. But for now, he focused on establishing himself in Fresno, where their first home was downtown at 260 South J Street in the town's residential area. They would remain there for about six or seven years before building an eight-room cottage on their new ranch at the top of Forthcamp (now Fulton Avenue) and eventually expanding it into a three-story mansion on a five-acre-block-sized estate at Olive and Wishon Avenues where Fulton now ends, beyond what was then the northern city limit.

The Wilson's first eight-room cottage on their ranch at the top of Forthcamp. Lorena and Paulette on bicycles in front. Rosanna in back of the fence at the stairs. Oscar, Jr on the porch.

Fresno was at the beginning of a peak growth period in 1887, described as " . . . one great real estate brokerage community; everyone almost a land seller" (Vandor 1919, Winchell 1933). George was no exception. He immediately became a real estate broker and general business agent in the office of Prusso and Wilson on J Street near his home. They specialized in country, grain, and stock farms; orchards; vineyards; and unimproved land. It was here that he began taking note of land opportunities he and Rosanna should invest in. Eventually, they would purchase four hundred acres north of and adjacent to the city limit with an eye to residential development, and vineyards in the outlying areas.

The population boom in Fresno generated an increasing need for housing which they both were keen to take advantage of. Within two years of moving here, he was writing friends in Colorado in an effort to persuade them to change their investments from mining to land in Fresno. He eventually set up his own office downtown. By definition, booms have a sunset, and

California's was no exception. The population in Fresno County peaked at 32,000 by 1890 with 10,900 living in the city. As activity slowed, his brother Frank left for San Francisco to begin a long career exporting lumber world-wide. It is possible that the decline of Sachs and Henghi and its eventual dissolution in 1897 was a catalyst for his move to the Bay Area, ending a career in general merchandising. Recognizing the nexus between his dreams of developing land and Frank's lumber company in San Francisco, George would later approach his brother in 1902 to work for Frank's company on commission bringing redwood to lumber yards in the Central Valley.

Oscar Wilson, Junior working the wagon with the horses in the Wilson's vineyard. ca 1890

Their youngest brother, Oscar, Jr., was the blue-collar worker in the family who became a plumber. Little is known about him—perhaps over-shadowed by his father and elder brothers—other than the fact that he lived with George and Rosanna briefly around 1900, while helping on their vast vineyard. If he ever wrote, no letters were saved. Correspondence between

Frank and George mention other friends and family members but rarely Oscar, Jr. What little mention they did make suggests their relationship with him was strained for unknown reasons. More frequently, they focused on lumber dealings and the possibility of importing lumber from Frank's company into the Central Valley through George.

Opportunity knocked on George's door again in the form of the 1893 Chicago World's Columbian Exposition. By then, Fresno was in a state of decline after the boom of 1886. The city's rapid descent started in 1890 and continued for the next five years.[17] Jumping on the opportunity to market the potential of the Central Valley to a global audience might very well turn things around. George saw the Chicago Exposition as a way to promote Fresno as a place to live and as a suitable environment for commercial agriculture. Thus, when talk began of sending an exhibit from Fresno to the exposition, he made sure he played a central role in organizing and managing this important marketing opportunity.

George Wilson, manager of Fresno's exhibit at the Chicago World's Columbian Exposition, 1893. Official photo.

The Wilson family around 1893. Rosanna was very short and her
feet needed to be on a box even when seated in photos.

The Fresno County World's Fair Commission elected him permanent secretary and superintendent of the Fresno exhibit in March of that year. He was given a monthly salary and railroad fare between Fresno and Chicago. It meant he would be in charge of the content of the displays and promotional material that would reach a world audience in the tens of thousands. It meant he had an expense-paid trip to Chicago where he could develop new contacts, promote Fresno, and visit relatives he had not seen in a very long time, if ever, in some cases. It also meant an eight-month absence from his family beginning in April 1893, when George left for Chicago with a trainload of exposition materials. Rosanna managed the household and the family business in his absence, often in the role of intermediary. He notified the bank in advance to honor her withdrawals, and Rosanna kept him informed of payment and taxes due dates, advised him on delinquent invoices, reported on relevant newspaper coverage, confirmed payments to the Kings River Lumber Company, and questioned whether to press tenants for overdue rents. At thirty-four, she was his partner in business.

Fresno County exhibit at the 1893 Chicago World's Columbian Exposition. Organized and managed by George.

California building at the 1893 Chicago World's Columbian Exposition.

The trainload of material for the exhibit included a giant redwood that would become the talk of the California Building, fresh produce, and a few things that made it back to the Wilson residence in Fresno in the end (e.g., painted porcelain vases, lidded glass display cylinders, and the gazebo in the center of the Fresno display). His initial letters home reflect the anxiety he felt upon his arrival in Chicago over the abysmally slow progress of fair organizers to complete the structure that would house Fresno's exhibit. He doubted that everything would be ready for the grand opening in May. When cold rain penetrated the unroofed buildings, he refused to unload the train car until the roof was completed. He found it difficult to secure reasonable housing, as landlords were raising the prices in anticipation of the crowds that would flock to the exposition. When he heard of the wreck involving the train coming from southern California, he worried that the car with his Fresno exhibit might have been damaged but was relieved to learn it was not in that train. When it finally arrived, he proudly reported that the Fresno shipment was packed so well in Fresno it reached Chicago pretty much intact. Upon his arrival, he anticipated being in Chicago for five to six weeks to get everything set up but would not have to spend the summer there. He severely underestimated his task.

On May 1, the fair opened to much fanfare. Two days later, George wrote to Rosanna describing the opening events: "All flags on the main building unfurled simultaneously." He thought the report that 400,000 attended was greatly exaggerated. All the fruit from Fresno looked good, helped by the cold weather. However, still there was no roof on the California building. Although some of the fruit was on display, he emphasized again that he was not putting everything out until the building was completed. The papers were reporting things happening that neither he nor anyone else he talked to saw. The weather continued to be bad—rain and snow. And he was not sure he wanted Rosanna to come out until it improved. He was already talking about bringing home gifts for everyone. For his son, Paulette, a chain for his watch; for Rosanna, Delfina, and Lorena, Turkish slippers; and for the family mantel, a large French plate mirror, four feet wide and five feet high, secondhand.

His letters home were frequent in May as he prepared the Fresno exhibit. "The little house is completed and the vases in place. . . . " He described the Ferris wheel and Buffalo Bill in detail and mentioned seeing his cousins. For the first time, he encountered "Blacks, Egyptians, and Arabs," whose cultural differences he could not abide. He emphasized that while he would like all the family to come to Chicago, they could not afford it. And he closed with a reminder to Rosanna to have his father, Oscar, attend to getting a mortgage. Likely a reference to the planning underway for the eight-room cottage on their new ranch.

June was a busy month at the exposition. Seeing the need to keep track of exhibit activity, George secured a brand-new hotel register to serve as a guest book that daily visitors to the California exhibit were urged to sign. Notable among them from his hometown were M. Theo Kearney, Louis Gundelfinger, W.O and J.A. Blasingame, J. W. Thompson, George C. Roeding, T. W. Patterson and his wife, Frank Burdick, J. P. Meux, Mr. and Mrs. J. Hull, S. N. Griffith, and J. Bingham.

Rosanna was lonely without George. She wrote to him that she missed him, especially on Sundays, because that was his day to be home with the family. They exchanged letters at least weekly, often long descriptions of the day with highlights of noteworthy events. Communication delays were inevitable in an era when letters had to travel by train back and forth between Fresno and Chicago. Both of them occasionally became impatient. In George's letters, if he was in a good mood, he would address her as "Dear Rosanna." But in response to her more terse letters, or long delays, he would defiantly begin with "Dear wife." She often included letters from Paulette and Lorena, thirteen and nine respectively, who were enthralled with their father's descriptions of Buffalo Bill and the Ferris wheel. But the attention of the children was often focused on the souvenirs they wanted their father to bring back. For Paulette, it was a money bank, a bicycle, and a "safety" that he repeatedly reminded his father to look for[18]; for Lorena, it was "bracelets, a ring, a brown winter dress, and blue Turkish slippers."

George let Rosanna know in a June letter that her half-brother, John Bautista Rogers Cooper, Jr. ("Johnie"), had been among the earliest visitors at the exposition. He wrote: " . . . Johnie Cooper is here alone . . . he has been to Mexico—he was very glad to see me. I told him you were down on weather, etc. . . . he says he does not think any of the gang will go to the fair. Martha can hardly get around, is not able to walk very well. . . . He does not want to have anything to do with the outfit." It is this half-brother whom Rosanna would confront years later in the dispute over the distribution of their father's estate.

To Rosanna's chagrin, George's letter-writing fell short in June as the business of the exposition accelerated, and she didn't hesitate to tell him so. She had sent him a scolding letter for not writing more often and included some pressed flowers from their garden as a reminder of home. In reply to her admonishment that he was not writing frequently enough, his lengthy response began with "Dear wife" instead of the usual "Dear Rosanna." He said he was writing as ordered and was quite upset by her disparaging comments. He dutifully went on to report on a show of lions, tigers, bears, dogs, and horses; more on the Ferris wheel that was one of the highlights of the exposition; and balloon rides. In an effort to assuage her concerns, George told her he had bought her "a peacock feather fan from Algeria for forty-five cents" and wanted to know what else she wanted him to bring home. However, feather fans and souvenirs were not going to diminish her curiosity about what her husband was doing in Chicago.

Her concerns increased to such a state that by the middle of June, she wrote him an imploring letter suggesting she come to Chicago so they could return together after the exposition ended. That got an immediate response! He said it was her decision, and if she wanted to make the trip, she should come by Union Pacific. Purchase a one-way ticket so they had flexibility on the return date. And be prepared for hot, humid weather far worse than hot but dry Fresno summers!

While Rosanna was concerned about George's activities away from home, her husband was concerned about money to support his trip and the sustained activity of the exhibit. Two months into his stay in Chicago, he worried about the lack of response from funders back in Fresno. He told Rosanna that if he did not get more money from the Fresno Commission, he was not going to stay long. Nonetheless, he asked her to find out what the round-trip fare was from Fresno to Chicago, in case the decision was for her to join him in there.

Sometimes, visitors from Fresno relied on George to arrange accommodations. Writing on letterhead from his office at Sachs & Heringhi on Mariposa Street, his brother, Frank, sent him a letter of introduction for Mrs. Meyer of Fresno, ". . . wife of Mr. Isaac Myer, who is a personal friend of mine. Please assist Mrs. Myer in securing hotel accommodations in Chicago and any other favors you may extend will be considered a great favor by Mr. Myer and myself." Further pressure for George who had a hard enough time finding accommodations for himself in a town where landlords were reaping the profits of escalated rents and hotel rates secured from exposition visitors with limited options for accommodations.

George had been gone for three months when, on July 23, Rosanna finally joined him in Chicago, drained of energy from days of nausea but eager to explore the fair. She needed time to recover before indulging in the excitement of seeing the exposition. Her letters to her children are filled with delightful descriptions of the electricity in the fountains, the Ferris wheel, fireworks, and exhibits so extensive that " . . . the distances between them are longer than Delfina's walks downtown" (about three miles from their new cottage on the outskirts of town up on Olive Avenue). She split her time between exploring them and staying with George at the Fresno exhibit to greet visitors that included dignitaries from Fresno and several of his relatives from the Midwest.

That month, George had sent home copies of the "Gold Dust" newsletter published by the California exhibitors. Printed in gold on diaphanous, pink-tinted paper, it described the California building and those involved in the Fresno exhibit, featuring George. The reactions of the two children could not have been more different. Thirteen-year old Paulette was ecstatic, but nine-year-old Lorena was unimpressed as they wrote to inform their mother of what they had received from their father:

"Papa wrote you a letter and he sent two pictures to you this morning, and he sent you two pink papers. Papa's and Miss Boyd's pictures were on each corner of the picture. Papa looked like he was running the whole World's Fair and Miss Boyd looked like she wasn't in it. The picture of the exhibit was there too. It was all done with gold dust. Tell Papa that I would like to have one of them with his picture on it. . . ." Letter from Paulette to Rosanna in Chicago describing the "Gold Dust."

" . . . [the 'Gold Dust' paper] was nothing important but I will save it for you." Letter from Lorena to Rosanna.

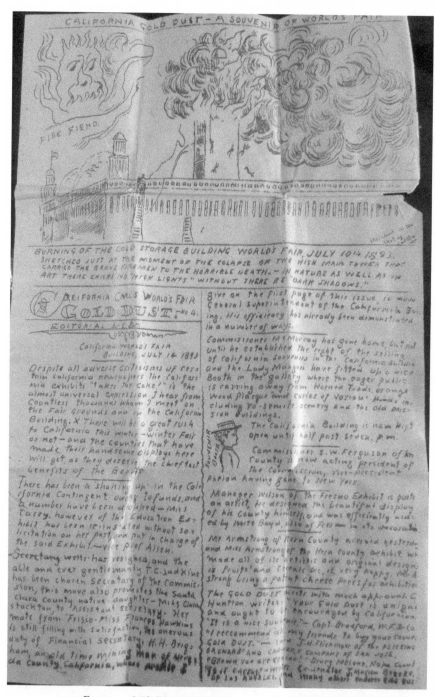

Front page of "California Gold Dust – a souvenir of World's Fair."

Paulette was a thirteen-year-old hyperactive boy. In addition to the feature article about his father and the Fresno exhibit, what may have caught his eye was the masthead with the artist's macabre rendering of bodies leaping off a burning building and the headline "Burning of the Cold Storage Building World's Fair, July 10, 1893. Sketched just at the moment of the colapse [sic] of the high main tower that carried the brave firemen to the [sic] horrible death. —In nature as well as in art there can be no 'high lights' without there be [sic] 'dark shadows.'"

In a family of prolific letter writers, Rosanna was far more descriptive in her coverage of the activities, and George was happy to defer to her epistolary abilities as he was drawn to the business at hand. She described for Lorena the beautiful embroideries and laces displayed in the women's building. She reported to Delfina on the cooking range that was as big as their entire kitchen in Fresno and the electricity in the fountains. In the meantime, George was laser-focused on the exhibit, connecting with visitors, and collecting business cards in anticipation of future networking. Among the visitors were various family members he was meeting for the first time in particular his father's brother, Austin Weir, mayor of Lincoln, Nebraska.

Back in Fresno, troubles were brewing at home. With both of his parents a long distance away, Paulette was acting out at every opportunity, and Delfina had no control. He was abusive to his sister, hung around with an unruly group, pulled up plants in the home garden, refused to do his schoolwork, and was generally uncontrollable. He needed a stronger hand to manage his exuberant outbursts than Delfina could offer. Long-distance letters of admonishment and threats—including not getting him the bicycle he so desperately wanted—were not achieving the desired effect. George was going to have to stay until the fair closed and afterward for as long as it took to load everything on a train car and accompany it back to Fresno. Reluctantly, in mid-September, Rosanna ended her visit to Chicago and returned alone to Fresno to take charge of problems back home with their son. The week of September 11, she changed her plans to visit Wisconsin and instead returned to Fresno alone after a month and a half at the world exposition.

Once in Fresno, she resumed the weekly letters to George. Her last letter to him on October 17 (just before he left Chicago) reveals their shared interest in their garden. She reported that the trees needed trimming but she would hold off so he could see them first. Bulbs were coming up. The verbena was not doing well. And folded in the pages of the letter—still there 124 years later—are the violets from their yard, a tangible memory of the value they placed on a lush garden.

The exposition closed at last on October 30. George had had to stay far longer than he initially expected. In his last short, brusque letter from Chicago on November 9—another "Dear wife" letter, upset with the lack of communication from Fresno—he wrote, "I now have the car half loaded and will complete it tomorrow and in all probability will start for home tomorrow afternoon via New Orleans. I do not know at this time at what time any train leaves. . . . The folks say you are very lovely and they don't know how I managed to get you. . . . " Reflective of the impression Rosanna had made on the people in Chicago, it was the only comment in any of his letters with a touch of romantic appreciation for his wife, saved for his last letter home before leaving Chicago on the train for Fresno.

George Wilson in his downtown office, seated at his desk. Mr. Davis on the left.

Having been immersed in the exposition virtually all of 1893, George returned home eager to resume his real estate business from his downtown office and to join Rosanna in planning for the residential development of their land and acquisition of additional acres. It was time to get out of the vineyard business. One of their first actions was to draw up the plans to expand the eight-room cottage built in 1892 at the southern edge of their ranch into a bigger house, now with the street address of 831 Olive Avenue at the end of Forthcamp.[19] However, house numbers were less helpful than general directions at a time when streets were missing, and the entire area was a flat plain in all directions. Thus, letters often came addressed to the Wilsons "at the north end of Forthcamp."[20] Correspondence between George and his brother, Frank, in San Francisco suggests that well in advance of moving into the big house, George had started to purchase special accessories for it. In one letter, he asked Frank to find him a bathtub, a special bathtub. Frank soon responded that he had indeed located the perfect tub—five foot five inches long with a drain and overflow, and three-inch rolled edges. New for twenty-eight dollars, or secondhand for twenty-five dollars.

Front entry to the Wilson estate at 831 Olive Avenue (at the "top of Forthcamp"). Hard pan was used to edge the driveway and walkways. George and one of his grandchildren are sitting on the front steps. Rosanna and Lorena are sitting on the porch to the right of the stairs. Their home was surrounded by gardens and fruit trees over the entire block.

Front of the house at 831 Olive Avenue. The gazebo from the Fresno County exhibit at the 1893 Chicago World's Columbian Exposition is visible in the distance on the other side of the yard.

The front entry inside the Wilson home at 831 Olive Avenue.

The living room of the Wilson home at 831 Olive Avenue.

Preserving the sentimental parts of the old cottage, they expanded the structure into a thirteen-room, three-story mansion with hallways, bathrooms, closets, beamed ceilings, natural pine trimmings, and French doors. The five acres of grounds were planted with eucalyptus to screen the house from the city that had expanded to their gate, citrus and fruit trees, and lush gardens.[21] The advertising brochure for the new tract would feature their cottage on the front cover and promote their estate as an example of the potential for attractive gardens.

Access to it was via a rail line laid up Forthcamp in 1909, running from the terminal at J Street and Divisidero along the west side of the Alhambra Tract owned by Delfina (and partners) and ending at the front gate of the Wilsons' ranch. The first car ride up Forthcamp was an eventful one, carrying guests up the unfinished line to the Wilsons' home for the wedding of their daughter Lorena Rose to George Weaver Huffman on June 17 (Winchell 1929).

George Weaver Huffman and Lorena Rose Wilson two years after their marriage.

The Roeding Park line added in 1912 provided an interesting feature reminiscent of a different era. Evening visitors who needed a ride back to the Olive and Forthcamp junction knew where to find the signal light attached to a transmission pole. As soon as the driver saw the light come on, he would trundle down the line to pick them up at no charge, regardless of whether they had arrived by car, buggy, or on foot.

Locating their own home at the top of Forthcamp (now Fulton) was a strategic move intended to attract growth northward and define the northern terminus of Forthcamp Avenue. If George could get A. G. Wishon, general manager of the San Joaquin Light and Power Company, to build his own mansion on the block across the street to the west (where the Tower Theatre now stands), the two residences would serve as anchors to the new community. They would be a visible gateway to affordable, high-class residences.

Unfortunately, this was one piece of the plan that did not fall into place and, as a result, created great consternation and embarrassment for the Wilsons.

Rosanna was about to turn forty in 1899 in the midst of exuberant planning for the move to a magnificent new home and anticipating development of their extensive land investments when she learned that her father was dying. She and Delfina rushed to his home in San Francisco only to be told by their stepmother, Martha, as she descended the stairs to meet them that they were too late. Their father had just passed away, and the estate was bankrupt. Sometime before John B. H. Cooper died on June 21 at the age of sixty-eight, he allegedly had gathered together Rosanna, Delfina, and his four children by Martha to let them know how he planned to divide up his estate among them. All six were to get a share of his land. Though Rosanna was confused now to learn that the estate may not have been everything she thought it was, in that period of grief, she let it go until another day. The thirteen years that had elapsed since she left the home her father had provided for her new family on his ranch in Castroville had passed by quickly, filled with many new adventures from Fresno to Chicago. Living in the Central Valley made it difficult to remain in contact with the only parent she appears to have stayed in touch with. The father who had protected her, who had given her land when she was but thirteen, and who had sent her away to school to learn English as his father had done for him. Her mother and that side of her family had receded further into the shadows of her past life. The ensuing disputes with her stepmother over land ownership and inheritance would not emerge for two more decades, and when they did, they would hit Rosanna like a gale-force wind, distancing her forever from the family she grew up with in Castroville. But for now, there was not even a cloud on the horizon. It was her trusted half-brother, John, Jr., who came to Fresno to offer his condolences and discuss the distribution of what was left of their father's estate on behalf of her stepmother, Martha. For the time being, the loss of her father was a momentary period of grief that would subside in the glow of enthusiasm she had for her first large land development in Fresno. If she had known then what she discovered later, she would have paid far greater attention to what John, Jr., was telling her. In the meantime, life went on as planned.

In 1908, they began subdividing their extensive ranch into sections starting with what would become the gateway to new residential neighborhoods, Wilson's North Fresno Tract. This was Rosanna's land and a project that would occupy her attention for the next three decades. She hired well-known Fresno County surveyor Scott McKay to survey the sixty acres and prepare the map that she submitted for approval a month later on November 16, 1908.[22] (See Appendix D.)

On October 26, 1908, at the same time Rosanna was working with McKay on plans for her Wilson's North Fresno Tract, George was trying to entice one of the prominent Fresno families looking for a new home location to consider the block across from his estate on Olive. He and A. G. Wishon entered into a formal agreement whereby Wilson would sell the entire Block 5 of the Wilson's North Fresno Tract where the Tower Theatre now stands (the block immediately west across the street from the Wilsons' estate) to Wishon for $1,000 on two conditions. First, the agreement required that Wishon improve the land by planting trees and shrubs in spring 1909 and have a landscape plan to show Wilson by January 1, 1909; and second, that Wishon have a plan for a "good, substantial dwelling house . . . to be placed on said premises so soon as the architect can prepare and furnish a plan thereof," according to original correspondence between A.G. Wishon and G.A. Wilson in the Wilson's private collection. Furthermore, the agreement explicitly stated that Wishon was expected to occupy the house as a family residence. Rumor had it that granting Wishon the entire block was in exchange for his agreement to construct the streetcar line that would service Rosanna's investment.

She counted on George's success negotiating Wishon's participation when she named the main street running through the tract Wishon Avenue. They were also counting on his participation when they wrote in the promotional brochure for the Wilson's North Fresno Tract: "Many of our leading citizens have already secured residence sites in this beautiful tract, one investor being Mr. A.G. Wishon . . . who has purchased a full block, and the plans for a handsome residence are in the hands of his architect."

However, two years later, there was still no Wishon house on Block 5. Although, on October 17, 1910, Wishon wrote it was still his intention to build such a house there, it never happened. Subsequently, Wishon loaned the block to the city for a public playground (Walker 1941). He never did follow through on the agreement and instead built his home on Huntington Avenue east of downtown Fresno. The street named for him was not changed and still carries that name to this day.

If their future residential development was to be successful, an important incentive for people considering moving north out of the downtown area was an easy means for commuting between home and work. Absent the automobile, a streetcar was the answer. In early 1908, George successfully negotiated with A. G. Wishon—perhaps in exchange for naming the street after him—for the Fresno Traction Company to build a double track line north up Wishon Avenue beginning at Olive and continuing to Carmen Avenue (just short of McKinley Avenue). (See Appendix D.) The extension of the "North Park Car Line" streetcar from downtown north up Forthcamp and jogging over to Wishon Avenue provided a way for residents to live in a quiet neighborhood well beyond the bustle of downtown. George deeded the right of way for the line and paid $7,000 in construction costs. In the thirty years since the Wilsons had arrived in Fresno, they had experienced the boom and decline of the 1880s and 1890s, and they were now positioned to take advantage of the next expansion in the early 1900s.

As if all this activity were not enough to keep them busy, George, always on the alert for lucrative opportunities, decided to invest in a banana plantation in Mexico with financial support from Rosanna. So, around the same time he was negotiating streetcar lines and Rosanna was working with the surveyor and the city planning the new residential development in Fresno as well as overseeing the construction of a second house in Santa Cruz, George bought a banana plantation in the State of Jalisco, Mexico, near what is today Puerto Vallarta, allegedly using early profits from the sale of lots in Rosanna's Wilson Tract.

George and Rosanna at their banana plantation in Mexico.

AP Wilson in the center with workers at the banana plantation.

Rosanna (left) with fresh pineapples at their banana plantation.

On August 9, 1905, George bought 31,667 shares of the Mexican Banana Company, later renamed the Mexican Tropical Fruit Company. He was the president and one of five directors and shareholders that included F. M. Roessler, T. E. Langley, L. L. Archibald, and S. M. Briscoe. George's only son, AP, was the secretary. It took a few years to get the plantation to the point where fruit was ready to ship, during which time George took a personal interest in the operational details. He and Rosanna scheduled their visits in January, sometimes accompanied by AP.

When it was finally time to secure a ship to import the bananas from Mexico, in September 1909, George and AP signed an agreement with S. A. Leffingwell to engage his Oakland-based ship to transport produce from Mexico to San Francisco. The ship was to pick up "bananas, green fruit, and other perishable produce" in Banderas Bay, Jalisco, Mexico, and transport it to San Francisco at intervals of twenty days. The northbound cargo would also include lumber and logs. Southbound out of San Francisco the ship would carry hay, lumber, laths, shingles, kerosene, and silk goods. It would make intermediate stops at ports along the way.[23] The arrangement was eerily reminiscent of the trading days of Rosanna's grandfather sailing his ship *The Rover* down the coast to Mexico and back with trade goods.

Civil unrest in Mexico laid waste to their plans. By July 1911, George was ready to sell the banana plantation and had retreated to Santa Cruz to avoid the valley heat, leaving his son in charge. However, AP reported from his office in Fresno that he had recently learned they had nothing to sell. Allegedly, Mexican revolutionaries had confiscated the plantation, and the manager mysteriously disappeared, purportedly murdered. Though the family lost a sizeable investment, George repaid all the investors—with Delfina's help. She made at least $30,000 (or about $760,400 in 2018) available to him, some of it from the profits on her investment in the Alhambra Tract. (See Appendix E.) Rosanna would forever warn her grandchildren never to go to Mexico though she never lost her appreciation of its culture and her connection to its history in Alta California.

As the sun set on their Mexican investment, attention returned to developments in Fresno that were in full swing now. But three dark clouds loomed on the near horizon, World War I, George's declining health, and troubles with Rosanna's inheritance. The impact on her would be harsh, in some ways devastating, yet they would open the door for her to emerge as a land baroness worthy of her heritage despite Grandmother Encarnacion's remonstrances to the contrary.

CHAPTER 3

LOSSES AND REBIRTH, 1915 TO 1947

At the bottom of a page in her small, private, pocket journal, there is a cryptic note written in Rosanna's hand: "M. Cooper H said I had their names taken off as I did not want them to appear there. By E.J.M."

George had been the driver in business ventures beyond Fresno and had helped Rosanna in some of her own dealings. For example, he led the negotiations to invest profits from their residential developments in the Mexican banana plantation. It was George who intervened with her uncle in the negotiations over Rosanna's and Delfina's share of land at Cooper Switch on her father's estate. It was George who allegedly decided that marriage would be too hard on Delfina and had the temerity to advise against it for her. A domineering, controlling man? Or the husband who simply assumed his expected role?

Shortly after the death of Rosanna's father in 1899, George's health began to visibly decline. When he could no longer work at his downtown office in the Forsyth Building, he worked from home. By 1913, he was under a doctor's care, and by 1914, he had been admitted to the sanitarium near St. Helena in Napa County, California—a premier health care facility at the time—known today as the Napa State Hospital. Quite a distance from Fresno, it was the best health care the family could get for him. Unfortunately, despite the excellent care, George would never recover. Just a few months after World War I erupted in Europe in the fall of 1914, George died from complications of diabetes (diagnosed at the time as Bright's disease) on January 14, 1915. Rosanna brought his body back to Fresno, where his funeral was held at their estate on Olive Avenue. He was buried in the family plot in nearby Mountain View Cemetery on Belmont Avenue. Perhaps knowing the end was near, in 1914, someone submitted his short biography to Ellis Davis for publication in the *Commercial Encyclopedia of the Pacific Southwest*. Although it attributes ownership of the Wilson Tract to George and his son, Rosanna was the actual landowner with a hands-on approach to managing her investment documented in land titles, deeds, and her own personal records. George assisted with the streetcar lines, and AP oversaw construction of several homes under the watchful eye of his mother until he left for Santa Cruz permanently.

A picnic on the Wilson ranch. Left to right: Lorena, Delfina, the Davis', George standing behind Rosanna seated. Prior to his hospitalization in 1915.

Rosanna in her forties. ca 1905

Rosanna was an unconventional woman with foresight, vision, and the energy to make things happen. As sad as she undoubtedly was about George's death in 1915, a door opened through which she stepped gracefully. As George's health had begun to fail, Rosanna had been assuming an increasingly more active role in land development and construction plans in Fresno and Santa Cruz. At the age of fifty-six, and over the next three decades, she went on to acquire a fortune in real estate and commercial property in Fresno's notable Tower District, building an estate worth ten times the value of what George had left her. More importantly, she created within her Wilson's North Fresno Tract a unique development that is today a registered historic district—the Wilson Island. She took a personal interest in the creation of the Wilson Island, a secluded section at the north end of the larger tract.

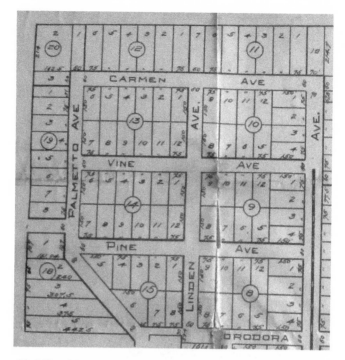

The Wilson Island portion of the original Wilson's North Fresno Tract. 1908

Entries in her pocket journal provide insights into her meticulous attention to the details of sales and construction. For example, she noted the width and length of each lot in the Wilson Island, when the mortgages (which she carried for many of the properties) were paid and released, and when transactions needed to be recorded in court. She tracked materials and labor costs. Either she was routinely near the building sites or someone was reporting the details to her. Perhaps both, as she lived but a few blocks away.

Her oversight and interests were not limited to activity in Fresno. In 1904, around the time she was moving into her new, big home on Olive in Fresno, she and her sister had purchased Lot 16 in Block C in the Kaye and Uhden Tract in Santa Cruz. On July 6, 1911, she applied to the city of Santa Cruz for a building permit to construct a residence on Riverside Avenue at a construction cost of $1,200 or about $30,000 in today's dollars. The cottage just off the San Lorenzo River near today's Beach Boardwalk was her tangible connection to a former life in Santa Cruz. She visited often, especially during the summers. Far from being an absentee landlord, she stayed on top of municipal activity that affected her property. In 1927, she was among the petitioners protesting the widening and paving of "The Esplanade" on Beach Street. The issue was taxation of the few to benefit the many.

After George's death in 1915, Rosanna actively took over all family business pursuits and created new ones. She conducted business from her office on the first floor of her home at 831 Olive Avenue, a short walk from the area she was developing. Not one to rely on banks, she put the payments and rent money she collected in a basket near the office door, periodically gathering them up and sending them with her granddaughter, Rosanna Katherine, to the bank to deposit. On one occasion, the young Rosanna carried $15,000 in cash down the street, a sum worth roughly $270,000 in 2018!

Rosanna inherited the thirst for development from generations of ancestors. During her formative years in Castroville and the Santa Cruz/Monterey area—from teenager to a young woman in her thirties—they were alive and actively involved in California and international business dealings around the Pacific Rim. As a young woman, she may have heard stories of her grandfather's voyages to Mexico, Hawaii, and China, or of his business dealings like the one in 1869 that leased part of his Sur Rancho for use as a dairy in exchange for $3,500 in gold coin.[24] When she was thirteen, her grandfather died, leaving the Castroville Ranch and a large portion of the El Sur Rancho along with its Spanish traditions to her father.

Even if she were not aware of specific operations, as a young girl living in the Cooper home, she may have been exposed to conversations about running the ranchos and California business politics. However, later events would reveal that she either was not present for these discussions or if she was, she did not fully understand the financial impact of numerous transactions. Tragically, it was not until she was in her late fifties that she would learn the full extent of the Cooper land holdings and the potential inheritance she believed trusted family members had withheld from her and Delfina. She would also learn that someone had altered mission baptismal records to hide her father's identity, thereby denying her position as the eldest daughter of John Baptist Henry Cooper.

For the next fifteen or twenty years following the death of her father in 1899, Rosanna did not give much thought to that conversation with John, Jr., when he came to visit her in Fresno back then about the distribution of their father's estate, but something never did feel quite right. So when the opportunity arose to bring up the subject of the missing will again in a chance conversation with the aging Martha on September 18, 1928, around the time she sold the El Sur Ranch, Rosanna got a perplexing and uncomfortable response from her clearly agitated stepmother, who refused to discuss it. The reaction motivated her to dig a little deeper for the truth and resulted in her filing a lawsuit. Inquiries with others led her to conclude that indeed there had been a will that was covered up.

According to her accounting filed in her court document, seventeen days after her father died on June 21, 1899, her half-brother John B. R. Cooper, Jr., came down from San Francisco to visit her in Fresno. Ostensibly, he came to convey his condolences, but there was another more urgent matter to be resolved unbeknownst to Rosanna, the rights of his children by Eduvigues as they affected the division of their father's estate. Rosanna had no reason to doubt John's news that their father had died intestate and that he and his mother, Martha, were trying to find a reasonable distribution under the circumstances. After all, only two weeks earlier, Martha had told them that the estate was bankrupt, so they did not expect much. It was a level of trust that would have devastating consequences for Rosanna.

JBHC and Eduvigues's common-law marriage meant there was a risk that their children had inheritance rights. The risk was not hypothetical for other reasons. The two girls had lived with JBHC and Martha in Castroville when they were young, were treated as his children, and in their original, unaltered baptismal records were officially recorded as his. In addition, Rosanna recalled that JBHC had made it clear earlier to everyone that he intended to divide his land among all six of his living children. John, Jr., and Martha must have been aware of the risk. Why else would Martha send John, Jr., to Fresno within seventeen days of his father's death with a proposal for Rosanna and Delfina, the two remaining children from JBHC's first marriage, to give up their inheritance rights in exchange for cash? Either JBHC had provided for his two daughters in his will or something else led their stepmother to believe they had a right to some portion of his estate. The proposal John, Jr., presented was that he and his mother would give Rosanna (who was acting on her sister's behalf as well) money in exchange for her and Delfina's agreement not to pursue any further claims against their father's estate. No one questioned how a bankrupt estate would come up with the money. It was contingent on the belief that her father had left no will and on her trust in her stepmother and half-brother to arrive at a fair distribution.

In the lawsuit that she ultimately filed, Rosanna claimed that in his visit with her on that Saturday, July 8, 1899, John, Jr., " . . . falsely and positively represented that their father had made deeds to all his real property, that he left no cash and no will, and that the will which he had theretofore made had been revoked, and that only the personal property remained to be administered." He further told her " . . . that his mother and himself proposed to make a liberal settlement with Rosanna and Delfina for their interests as heirs in the personal property . . . and to give them more than their share." They were presented with documents to sign which allegedly " . . . conveyed to J.B.R. Cooper [John, Jr.] 'all real property in the State of California of which J.B.H. Cooper, deceased, was ever at any time seized or possessed.'"

In exchange, she and Delfina would each receive $2,500 in cash and a note for $2,000 signed by J.B.R. Cooper, Jr., and Martha M. Cooper. Once John, Jr., had their agreement that Saturday, he moved quickly. He was a twenty-seven-year-old lawyer who, as a coexecutor of the estate with his mother, knew that his portion of the inheritance would be positively affected with a reduction in the number of heirs among whom it would be divided. He recorded their signed documents immediately the following Monday, July 10, 1899. In other words, Rosanna had signed away her inheritance rights as one of six surviving children of John B. H. Cooper to an estate valued at the time to be worth $400,000 to $500,000. Martha had now ensured that the estate would be divided only among herself and her own four children.

By the time Rosanna filed the lawsuit, she was angry with her stepmother and half-brother and hurt by the thought that she had been duped by people she trusted. Her feelings are reflected in her accounting of the meeting with her half-brother in Fresno that Saturday in 1899, when she said " . . . [John] asked [her] to trust him and his mother and promised that he would look after all their interests, and that he and his mother would, as administrators of [their father's] estate, take charge of everything pertaining to [Rosanna's and Delfina's] rights and interests better than they or any other person could do, reminding [them] of the fact . . . that he was acquainted with the law, and that he knew the situation and was in a position to protect [their] rights and interests in all respects." He concluded by telling them " . . . that the employment of any attorney by them would be a useless and unnecessary expense, and besides that, it would lead to undesirable publicity." An edgy conclusion to an otherwise positive conversation. Publicity for whom? Dragging the estate of a prominent Californian through a court battle would certainly be unpleasant for everyone. But perhaps it was a veiled threat to reveal their status as children of a common-law marriage in an era when that would have been personally embarrassing to them.

This is only one side of a complicated story. However, based on other court documents filed by Martha Cooper and her son, John B. R. Cooper, Jr., it would appear that Rosanna may have been correct in believing she had been duped by her stepmother and half-brother. Contrary to what John, Jr., told her on his visit to Fresno, according to the probate record for the estate of their father, J. B. H. Cooper, there had indeed been a will that John, Jr., and his mother presented to the court on July 25, 1899, for processing, only fifteen days after he filed Rosanna's signed agreement to give up her inheritance rights in exchange for $4,500 in cash and persuading her that no will existed. The record goes on to state that all property was now in the hands of Martha and John, Jr., and that proper notice had been given to all heirs who were present in court a year later on June 29, 1900, assenting to the distribution of the property and the closing of the estate. All heirs save two. The heirs present that day were Martha, the administrator of his estate, and "his only descendants," John B. R. Cooper, Jr. (coexecutor with his mother), Abelardo E. Cooper, Alfred H. G. Cooper, and Alice F. Dillon (née Cooper). If John and Martha failed to mention the court date to Rosanna, it was presumably not an oversight. Rosanna's and Delfina's absence, if in fact they were mentioned in their father's will, would not have been questioned anyway since they had agreed to give up any claim on their father's property by signing the agreement John, Jr., had presented the year before. Martha and her four children returned to their home in San Francisco at 1926 Octavia Street (a block from the intersection of Gough and California Streets) that day comfortable with the knowledge that they had retained all of the vast desirable land and property of one of the largest landholders in the state for themselves. They also believed that the $9,000 it cost to settle affairs with Rosanna and Delfina was a liberal settlement, more than the women were entitled to.

Their stepmother and half-siblings inherited "all the property in the hands of [Martha and John, Jr.] . . . acquired before J. B. H. Cooper's marriage to Martha . . . " Mentioned specifically were: shares of Rancho Bolsa del Portero y Moro Cojo, property in Castroville, a lot in the City of Monterey lying near the old Custom House, 765 head of cattle, 42 head of horses, and sundry other items. A search of property deeds would confirm if the Castroville property also included the lots between Merritt Street and the Tembladero Slough that J.B.H. Cooper had given his daughters Rosanna and Delfina when they were children. Notably absent was any mention of the El Sur ranch, which apparently Martha had sold either for her own benefit or in response to the bankrupt condition the estate was allegedly in.

Whether or not a will would have resulted in a different outcome is unknown, along with her father's intentions for his two daughters. But Rosanna was clearly disadvantaged by the lack of access to information that might have resulted in a different outcome. We'll never know, as the voices closest to the truth fell silent decades ago. Unfortunately, the will may not have survived the destruction of public records pertaining to the estate in the fires after the San Francisco earthquake of April 1906. It took Rosanna a while to regroup and gather the momentum to file her lawsuit. By the time she did, the value of her father's estate had increased to $650,000 to $700,000, roughly equivalent to $9 million in 2018.

Rosanna lost her lawsuit on appeal. In 1932, the judge upheld the lower court decision that she had had her chance to contest the offer in 1899 and didn't take it. The purpose here is not to defend either side of the story or the fairness of the distribution of her father's estate. It is about what Rosanna did next and how she translated her anger into actions that ultimately resulted in the substantial estate she built and her legacy to Fresno. She may well be the Cinderella of this tale who emerged victorious from the apparent efforts of a stepmother motivated to deny her existence.

It hardened her resolve in tangible ways, reflected ultimately in what she created in her land developments. But first, she wanted to forget the Coopers. Her granddaughter, Rosanna Katherine Huffman (RKH), was twenty-one at the time her grandmother received the final court decision at their home on the family estate at the corner of Olive and Wishon. RKH recalled her grandmother returning from meetings at the coast quite angry, telling her, "It's all lies." And most unforgettable, her grandmother gathering a lot of documents, putting them in a bag and telling RKH to burn them all. Presumably these included correspondence from her father and other things that were painful reminders of the family she had left behind in Castroville and that she now believed had betrayed her.

father's estate. Right: Delfina around the same time.

As Rosanna was working through the angst of dealing with the inheritance issues, Delfina's health began to fail. Rosanna's close confidante and occasional business partner who had lived with Rosanna and her family her entire adult life was fading. They were inseparable their entire lives. Delfina's health was never robust, some say due to a goiter. Photos of her reveal a thin woman with dark circles under her eyes. As early as age seventeen, still living with her father and stepmother in Castroville, her stepmother wrote to a family member that she had been urged by Delfina's father to take her with her on a trip south to Anaheim. "He thinks it will do Delfina good. She is not well." Fourteen years later, when she was living with the Wilsons in Fresno and Rosanna was away in Chicago, Rosanna's daughter, Lorena, wrote to her mother that Aunt Delfina was having "the blues" and headaches. Whatever the problem, Rosanna was uncomfortable enough leaving her children with Delfina that she arranged for Grandfather Oscar (George's father) to look in on them regularly. He was nearby, just south of them on the west side of Forthcamp near the canal. Perhaps it was because of Delfina's poor health that George did not think it was a good idea for her to marry. Whether for lack of suitors or poor health, she remained a spinster, living the rest of her life with her sister's family, either in Fresno or at the house she and Rosanna built in Santa Cruz.

As a young child, Delfina was known for her rebellious nature at boarding school in Santa Cruz. As an adult, poor health did not stop her from actively engaging in her own real estate investments, in particular the Alhambra Tract just southeast of Rosanna's Wilson's North Fresno Tract. The forty-acre Alhambra Tract included moderate, affordable housing. It is where Delfina made her money beginning in 1910 by selling lots to families who would then build their own homes. The tract is bordered by Olive on the north and Elizabeth on the south, between Forthcamp (now Fulton) and Glenn. Residential lots were primarily along College, Poplar, and San Pablo. (See Appendices D and E, original maps of Wilson's North Fresno Tract and Alhambra Tract.) At the time of her death in 1929, Delfina still owned thirty lots on five different blocks in the tract.

Delfina was creative, expressing herself musically and artistically. At seventeen, she wrote the music for Rosanna's wedding reception, and in 1897, she wrote the "Ramona Waltz," published by the Union Mutual Music Company of New York.

Cover page of the "Ramona Waltz" composed by D. E. Cooper.
Union Mutual Music Co. New York. 1897

It was through her artistic endeavors that she easily cultivated a wide network of friends. Her involvement in her community was reflected in the headline of her obituary and its placement on the front page of *The Fresno Morning Republican*, "Fresno club woman dies." She was well known by many of Fresno's oldest families, indeed a woman who was a prominent Fresno resident exemplified by her membership in the prestigious Parlor Lecture Club since 1911 (as was Rosanna), where she played an active role in its art department. She oversaw decorating the Parlor Lecture Club's floats for two years, during which time they took first prizes in the Raisin Day Parade.

Delfina's passing on August 5, 1929, at age sixty-seven at their summer cottage in Santa Cruz was the third significant loss for Rosanna. First she lost the father who had virtually raised her from childhood; then her husband, who partnered with her in numerous business adventures; and now the sister who was at once the touchstone with her past and the one person—perhaps the only person—who garnered her implicit trust as they suffered through the ordeal of her father's estate, the one person with whom she had lived virtually her entire life. The sister who might have been left behind with their mother long ago had it not been for Rosanna's constant crying and pleas to her father to bring Delfina too. They had shared a tumultuous childhood in Castroville that may well have been occasionally the subject of their quiet conversations in Spanish as adults. The love that bonded them together was uninterrupted. Rosanna relied on Delfina to watch over her children when she was occasionally away despite concerns about her frail health. When Delfina died, Rosanna lost a trusted confidante. It was such a loss that she sold the cottage at 223 Riverside Avenue in Santa Cruz, her last remaining connection to the world of their childhood, and had Delfina's body returned to Fresno, where she is buried in the Wilson family plot.

Rosanna at the hotel in London, age 70. 1930

Rosanna needed to get away; she needed to reset her compass. Her solution was a trip to Europe, presumably using in part money she inherited from Delfina. Thus it was on May 3, 1930, seven months after the stock market crash that kicked off the Great Depression and a month after she finalized her sister's estate, at the age of seventy, she gathered up her daughter, Lorena Rose Huffman, and her two granddaughters, Rosanna Katherine and Evelyn Delfina, and boarded a train in Fresno for a four-month grand tour of Europe. Given her prior experience with daily nausea back in 1893 on the train ride to meet George in Chicago, she may not have been thrilled about the first segment of their excursion. It took six days from Fresno through Los Angeles, New Orleans, and Washington to finally reach New York City. Arising early the next morning, they boarded the *SS Cedric* for an eight-day crossing of the Atlantic. The destination was Liverpool, where they were met and ushered through customs to the train for London. The glamorous First Avenue Hotel in High Holborn, London, was their home base from which they explored the British Isles. For the next seven days, they toured Ireland, England, and Scotland before leaving London on June 8 by train for the night boat crossing to Holland. Once on the continent, travel was by car, often accompanied by a guide. Each of the next twenty-two days was a different destination, sometimes with multiple stops a day to take in castles, galleries, historic, and scenic sights of the Low Countries, Hungary, Germany, Switzerland, and Austria. The finale was a month on the road with a guide entering Italy through the Alps, visiting the Mediterranean and moving on to the castles of France. The trip culminated with a special guided tour of Paris before heading back to Liverpool for departure on the *SS Britannia* on August 30. Another six-day train ride, this time via Niagara Falls, Chicago, Salt Lake City, and San Francisco brought the four ladies home at 11:40 p.m. on a sultry Saturday, September 13. Rosanna and her entourage were exhausted after traveling nonstop for fourteen days by ship and train to reach home in Fresno. Though the reporter erred on the dates, the tone of the article in the *Fresno Republican* on September 30, 1930, accurately reflects the enthusiasm of the girls sharing highlights of their adventure upon their return:

> Mrs. G.H. Wilson [sic] and Mrs. G. W. Huffman and two daughters, Misses Rosana [sic] and Evelyn Huffman, returned home Sunday night from an extended trip abroad, having left here May 2. They sailed from New York for Queenstown, Ireland, and, after several weeks in England and Scotland, went to Holland, Belgium, Germany, Denmark, France, Austria, Czechoslovakia, Hungary,

Italy, and Switzerland. They were in Naples during the di-
saster, and Mrs. Huffman and Miss Evelyn Huffman had
the experience of climbing part way up Mount Vesuvius
at the time lava was flowing from it on the opposite side.

Rosanna's two children could not have grown into two more different
people. Albert Paulette, known as Paulette in his youth and AP as an adult,
was notorious for his wild character throughout his life.

AP Wilson at about age 13 on his new bicycle near the Fruit Avenue entrance to their ranch.

Rosanna never fully trusted him as an adult. She never allowed him to
handle the financial side of her real estate developments, though she did
rely on him to obtain building permits and oversee construction to some
degree. When as a young man of thirty he married Mabel Amanda Barley,
allegedly an actress from San Francisco, the family considered it yet another indication of his flamboyant character.

Mabel Amanda Barley, AP's wife

It was probably around the time of his marriage that he had a small house built at 1279 Wishon across the street from the big Wilson home at Olive and Wishon where he had grown up and just north of where the Tower Theatre stands today. He later had the blue-and-white cottage-style house moved a mile farther north to a small triangular lot on the northeast corner of Wishon and Michigan just south of the railroad tracks at Shields, where it remained until it burned down around 2000.

The house AP Wilson built at 1279 Wishon and moved to this location later south of Shields Avenue. It has since burned down.

AP had continual financial problems that put his house at risk on several occasions and was rescued more than once by his mother or aunt. He often spent the warm Fresno summers at the family cottage in Santa Cruz and around 1925 moved to his own home there permanently. Having been coached by his father in a career in real estate, he first tried setting himself up in that business with a partner, C. M. Anson.[25] His love of cooking led to a brief foray into the restaurant business in Santa Cruz, where he died a short time later in 1931 at the age of fifty a year after his Aunt Delfina passed away. Any property he was to inherit from her in 1930 was conveyed instead to his mother, likely in compensation for her earlier financial help. She kept close track of the construction finances on the lots he managed while he assisted her initially with the development of the Wilson Island, keeping him under her wing. She noted when she paid him commissions on lot sales and how much; labor and materials costs on the construction sites he was overseeing; when she loaned him money, the amounts, and whether they were repaid; and she covered the final costs of his phone and power bills at his Fresno house when he left for Santa Cruz in 1925.

Lorena Rose Wilson in her teens.

She had quite the opposite relationship with her daughter, Lorena Rose, who continued to live with Rosanna and George in Fresno at the Wilson estate on Olive Avenue following her marriage to George Weaver Huffman in June 1909.

George Weaver Huffman

George Weaver Huffman's pool hall in Fresno.

In the eyes of her parents, their son-in-law's only flaw was his investment in the pool hall downtown. Lorena Avenue in Fresno is named for the daughter she admired. Lorena was Rosanna's only child who bore grandchildren whom she adored.

Rosanna's grandchildren, L to R: George Wilson, Evelyn Delfina, and Rosanna Katherine Huffman. ca 1917

Rosanna's grandchildren, L to R: Rosanna Katherine, George Wilson, Evelyn Delfina Huffman. ca 1921

The first one, her namesake, Rosanna Katherine Huffman, born November 21, 1911, was the quiet violinist who grew up listening to Rosanna's stories of her early life and, in her later years, was keen to share her grandmother's history, especially as it related to early California. Her second grandchild, George Wilson Huffman, was born February 15, 1914. In his youth, he was a star tennis player, winning the Fresno Bee Junior Tennis Tournament Championship in 1929, and later went on to serve as municipal court judge in Fresno for twenty-seven years. Rosanna described her third grandchild, Evelyn Delfina, born April 10, 1916, as enthusiastic, talkative, and inspired by the world around her on their European trip in 1930. It was Evelyn who spotted the young actor on their ship to London and from that point on remained infatuated with the glamour of their excursion.

George Weaver Huffman in his office when he was a municipal court judge in Fresno.

About that cryptic note, Rosanna entered in her personal journal: "M. Cooper H said I had their names taken off as I did not want them to appear there. By E.J.M."

Who was M. Cooper H? Most likely it was Rosanna's stepmother, Martha, who preferred to be known as Martha Cooper Hughes after 1918, when she married her third husband, James Joseph Hughes.[26] It was sometime after 1918 that the firestorm erupted when Rosanna and Delfina contested the distribution of their father's estate. There are lots of things on, or at which Martha might not have wanted them to appear during that time. Whatever it was, Rosanna made a point of entering the notation in her personal journal because she believed M. Cooper H was indeed Martha, and the reference was to her and her sister.

"E.J.M" was Rosanna's uncle, Eusebius Joseph Molera, with whom at one time George had been in business and with whom George had communicated on Rosanna's behalf during the period when they were trying to resolve ownership of the land at Cooper Switch following the death of her father. Eusebius was Martha's brother-in-law, which may have put him in a position to be privy to Martha's thoughts regarding Rosanna and Delfina, whose relationships with their stepmother had soured permanently after the turmoil of the lawsuit, if not well before. They were the living reminders of that portion of her deceased husband's past that she was more than willing to have history forget.

Though we will never know for certain who Martha was referring to by "them" or what she wanted "them" excluded from, someone with influence over the Cathedral San Carlos Borromeo clergy in Monterey did have the baptismal records altered for JBHC's daughters from his first marriage. The name of both Rosanna and Delfina's father, Juan Cooper, was crossed out in heavy black ink to hide his identity, and their surname of Cooper was scratched out and overwritten with Soto. Written over their father's name in Spanish is "father unknown" in the case of Rosanna's and "N.N." (short for "unnamed") on Delfina's. Interestingly, by the time of Rosanna's marriage in 1879 and that of her sister Guadalupe in 1882, JBHC was back in the records as the father of both girls. Speculation as to who arranged for the baptismal alterations might point to Martha, who was eager to be married in the Catholic Church and may have seen the existence of a first wife and children as an impediment. If so, the alternation was made around 1870 or 1871, near the time of her marriage to JBHC. When the girls were marrying a decade later, it was a moot issue, so there was no risk in correctly identifying their father in their marriage records. Martha was well known for her considerable charitable contributions to the Catholic Church, which had allegedly earned her a papal medal in 1937. At the time of this writing, neither Rosanna nor Delfina—or for that matter their mother, Eduvigues (JBHC's first wife), or their other sisters—were acknowledged in the Cooper genealogy on the wall at the Cooper-Molera adobe in Monterey.[27] A decade out of the life of JBHC wiped clean and a family expunged.

Sadly, the exclusion of his first child, Rosanna, is an unfortunate loss to the Coopers and Vallejos, the consequence of personal rivalries and intense emotions over parentage and status, belied by the facts. What Rosanna achieved in her lifetime is a measure of the same love of the land and will to succeed that motivated her forefathers. Ironically, while the individual homes of Rosanna's grandfather, father, and stepmother are listed on historic registers, noted for their architectural contributions and the prominence of the owners, it was JBHC's daughter Rosanna who left not a single home but an entire neighborhood of seventy-eight homes—significant both individually and collectively because of the period in our history they represent, the distinctive architectural styles, and the prominence of the original owners. They are visible evidence of Rosanna's intentional positive influence on the expansion of residential development in Fresno in the first decades of the 1900s. She was a risk-taker who valued the potential of investing in land and who fell in love with an adventurer. She was indeed her father's—and her mother's—child.

Rosanna Cooper Wilson remained active in Fresno and Santa Cruz until her death on July 14, 1947, at the age of eighty-eight after breaking her hip in a fall three years earlier walking down the street. She was a Native Daughter of the Golden West and a lifetime member of the Parlor Lecture Club, as was her sister Delfina. At the time of her death, the estimated value of her estate was $319,396 (equivalent to $3.6 million in 2018). Ironically, the majority of that was in land, not cash, as had been the case with her father's estate according to her half-brother, whom she doubted her entire life. If true, history appears to have repeated itself. She left not only an historic treasure worthy of the attention given to the historic landmarks of her forefathers, but, to the homeowners, she left the ongoing care and nurturing of a small piece of California. She is buried next to George in the Wilson family plot in the Mountain View Cemetery in Fresno—not far from where she lived the majority of her life—along with her sister and daughter . . . among others, with the exception of her son, AP.

She will always be remembered for the wonderful stories she told of California sea otters (a nod to her grandfather's business escapades in the 1840s), for the lullabies in Spanish she sang to her children and great-grandchildren, and for her stories of life in the Pajarao and Salinas coastal valleys in the 1800s where she grew up. If only her granddaughter Evelyn, long ago had been able to figure out how to work the wax recording device she purchased (the only thing available at the time) expressly to preserve her grandmother's unique character.

CHAPTER 4

HER VISION:
A SECLUDED NEIGHBORHOOD WITHIN
AN EASY COMMUTE TO DOWNTOWN

Fresno was ripe for residential expansion in the early 1900s. The *Fresno Morning Republican* (January 5, 1908) reported extremely high demand for more housing for families of modest incomes. The story estimated that hundreds of "cottages" could be rented or sold if available. City leaders were concerned that the scarcity of housing was causing families to leave the area in large numbers. "Demand is strongest for modern places; cottages of six or seven rooms. Most all buildings here over five rooms go into two-story houses, and so are not available for this demand." So many families were looking for homes that businessmen called the demand "the largest which has been experienced in this city in the past fifteen or sixteen years. From the indications, it is predicted that the coming spring is to be the greatest ever in the real estate business."

Rosanna's sixty-acre parcel of land north of downtown was perfectly positioned to meet this demand. In October 1908, she hired notable Fresno County Surveyor Scott McKay to complete a subdivision map of Wilson's North Fresno Tract, which she filed the following month. Her plan for a residential neighborhood met Fresno's needs in two ways. Part of it catered to the demand for small cottages, and part of it served a very different clientele. (See Appendix D, Wilson's North Fresno Tract map.) Interest in residential neighborhoods that provided a secluded area for wealthier homeowners grew in the early twentieth century. Rosanna designed a section that responded to this interest by configuring the streets at the northern end of her tract to create an interior island for larger homes of the wealthy. That secluded area, now known as the Wilson Island, is one of only four registered historic districts in Fresno as of this writing. The homes in the island are a collection of distinctive architectural styles including Craftsman bungalows, Prairie, Tudor, Spanish Revival, Mission Revival, and French Norman Revival. Almost two-thirds of them were completed before the Great Depression, but the first vigorous construction boom kicked off in 1919 when 15 percent of the homes in the Wilson Island were completed in that single year. With her husband and son as her agents, she advertised that Wilson's North Fresno Tract was "destined to be one of the highest class districts around the city."

"Fresno, 1916, east of drill tower on S. P. Railroad reservation." Vandor, 1919

When Rosanna bought the land, she was taking a calculated risk. There was virtually nothing yet that far north of downtown. To put this tract in context, imagine an era in the early 1900s when the homes and businesses of the twenty-five thousand people living in the city of Fresno were located primarily downtown, well south of Divisidero along Fulton and Van Ness (then J and K Streets). At the time, people complained that the original Fresno High School built in 1896 on O Street between Tuolumne and Stanislaus Streets was too far out of town.[28] Belmont was the northernmost street labeled on the 1906 Fresno city map. And the farthest thing noted north of Belmont was a berry farm just below Olive. Rosanna was investing in the future. It proved to be a good investment. In 1921, thirteen years after her 1908 filing of the subdivision, Fresno High School moved farther north just beyond her tract to its current location on Echo at McKinley, reinforcing residential expansion to the north of downtown.

Wilson's North Fresno Tract included twenty individual blocks. Rosanna took a personal interest in the northern most eleven blocks which became the secluded island she envisioned would become a suburb for the wealthy. Within the area bordered by Echo, Wishon, Carmen, and Floradora, she named the streets, invested in building a few houses for immediate sale, and carried the deeds on twenty-four of the properties. She also noted details in her pocket journal about surrounding streets—the length of Olive and Wishon Avenues, future easements on McKinley, and major electrical infrastructure. She anticipated building out future commercial spaces, one of which was Fern Avenue. In the 1940s, that street was the northern border of their fenced estate on the last remaining vacant portion of the original tract. She created the new street in 1946 at a cost to her of $7,000 so commercial buildings could be added that would generate income for her family. She planned the street to be wider than normal, seventy feet instead of the usual sixty feet.

Under her guidance, she and AP directly oversaw the construction of at least eleven of the seventy-eight historic homes. She often dealt directly with notable architects working on the Wilson Island homes such as Shorb and Meade, and Taylor-Wheeler. For example, in her pocket journal she noted on October 25, 1919, $15,215 due to eight people, among them Dan Shorb.

She negotiated with Fresno County for special water rates as compensation for her bearing the cost of installing water pipes. In a 1931 letter to the county superintendent, who apparently was going to raise her water rate, she argued that she was entitled to a rate reduction as part of a contract with the county. She wrote:

> I have no concession for water, but a contract with the water company at 8 cts per 1000 cu. ft. and that on my part I have paid a couple of very valuable considerations for said contract, one of them being some 6041 lineal [sic] ft. of 4 inch water pipe furnished and laid by me at quite some expense, which pipe has come into your possession. The other consideration does not concern you as it has not passed into your hands.
>
> The yearly interest on the amount paid by me for pipe and installation, (for which I have not been reimbursed) will be about three times the amount yearly that I save by the 8 cent rate, so you see that the Contract has been a rather expensive one for me.
>
> In other words this 8 cent rate has cost me about $120.00 per year for over 22 years, and I save about $40.00 per year by the 8 cent rate, leaving a deficit of about $80.00 per year, on Pipe alone.

Not a shrinking violet, she let the supervisor know she would not back down when she concluded: "Kindly let me hear from you further, and if you wish to rescind this Contract, write me a letter to that effect, and I will know what steps to take in the matter."

The deeds she issued for lots in the Wilson Island reveal how she intended to create the feeling of exclusivity. First, she stipulated the minimum construction cost. She knew exactly how much it cost to build a home of a specific size. So, when she included minimum construction cost in her deeds, she knew precisely what she was asking for. Typically, smaller homes on lots along Wishon had a minimum required building cost of $1,500, more consistent with the cost to build a modest cottage in 1920. At that time, self-built homes could be purchased for about $1,200. However, lots in the Wilson Island would host grander homes. She required builders to submit designs for homes that cost minimally between $3,500 and $8,500 to construct (equivalent to $46,000 to $111,000 in 2018). If she could attract the right buyers, profits would be high. For example, the original deed she issued for the lot at 660 Carmen Avenue stipulated a construction cost of $6,500 (about $85,000 in 2018). It was sold by the builder in 1924 at a price of $23,000 (about $328,000 in 2018), four times the construction cost. That particular sale was reported on the front page of the *Fresno Republican* as "one of the biggest sales of residential property in Fresno that year," and local realtors considered it an indication that Fresno was coming out of the agricultural depression and "back into her own."

Next, Rosanna required the houses and outbuildings to be set back far enough from the street to create large front yards. On lots that were typically 75 feet wide and 150 feet deep, the house had to be at least twenty-five feet from the street and the "stable or barn" seventy-five feet[29], plenty of room to plant the large deodar cedar trees, many of which are still there almost a hundred years later. Today, the Wilson Island is noted for its mature landscapes and tree-lined streets.

Special features were included in many of the homes. In some of the larger homes, architects incorporated card and billiard rooms befitting the social status of the early buyers. Interiors were adorned with such eccentricities as indoor atriums, chandeliers imported from Europe, and fireplaces made of tiles fabricated by the notable Arts and Crafts tile maker of the era, Ernest Batchelder, whose tiles were shipped throughout the United States from his workshop in Pasadena, California. Perhaps it was on his trip through Fresno around that time that Rosanna made his acquaintance and learned of the tiles. Today, the Wilson Island homes that have Batchelder fireplaces are included in the inventory of his works maintained by the Pasadena Historical Museum.

Example of fireplace tiles made by Ernest Batchelder found in several Wilson Island homes.

There were restrictive covenants, typical of the era as well, but one in particular was unique to Fresno. Rosanna's deeds included the stipulation that the buyers agree: " . . . not to sell or lease said property, or any part thereof, nor to convey by deed or otherwise any portion of said property, excepting to persons belonging to the Caucasion race; and agree not to sell, lease, convey, or otherwise dispose of the whole, or any portion of said property to any person born in the Turkish Empire, nor to any lineal descendant of such person, nor shall any such person occupy said premises." In other words, Armenians were excluded.

This was the period of the Armenian diaspora, driven out of Asia Minor under the dark cloud of genocide organized by the Ottoman state. Drawn to Fresno's rich agricultural land and Mediterranean climate, by the time Rosanna was launching the Wilson Island, they represented the largest minority population in town and dominated raisin production. Whereas early arrivals had started as migrant workers, by the 1920s, they were becoming land owners. Unfortunately, they were not welcome in the Wilson Island. The vision was to attract Fresno's elite white business community. Perceived detractors were excluded. Fortunately, such restrictive covenants are no longer legal, and the modern neighborhood of the Wilson Island reflects the cultural, ethnic, and racial diversity of the Fresno metropolitan area.

One more aspect of the strategy used by the Wilsons to interest wealthy colleagues in the new development was the location of their own home. Rosanna and her husband built their own three-story mansion on the block in the southeast corner of Wilson's North Fresno Tract. Their estate took up the entirety of Block 4, the largest block in the tract, bordered by Olive on the south, Wishon on the west, Paloma[30] on the north, and Moroa on the east. Moroa was named after the daughter of one of George's friends and was initially spelled with an "o" until it was later mistakenly changed to Maroa, the spelling used since about 1925.

Their home and grounds were grand. The granite front porch stretched from side to side, and from the granite stairs leading up to the house, you could see the streetcars traveling up Forthcamp from downtown. The gazebo that George used at the 1893 Chicago World's Fair was prominently displayed in the front yard. Citrus trees dotted the landscape, and small, thin blocks of hardpan were used to edge planters. Eventually, when additional space was needed for the northbound Forthcamp streetcar to make the sharp turn west on Olive before turning right to continue north up Wishon, Rosanna would sell a slice of their block to the city for a widening (in front of what is now the Chicken Pie Shop and since filled in).

One last piece of the marketing plan was for A. G. Wishon to build his home on Block 5, directly across from the Wilson home. It never happened, even after public announcements that it was part of the new development.

Yet the main street in the tract is still called Wishon Avenue, after the man who is most often associated with the San Joaquin Light and Power Company, predecessor to Pacific Gas and Electric. A.G. Wishon was also the vice president, manager, and director of the Fresno Traction Company and in that capacity worked with George Wilson on the extension of the streetcar lines up Wishon Avenue, cutting right through Wilson's North Fresno Tract.

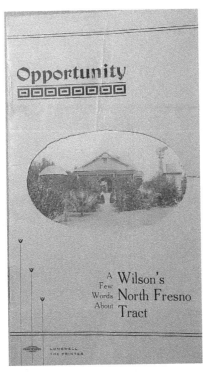

The original sales brochure for the Wilson's North Fresno Tract, printed around 1895, featured the Wilson's cottage on the front cover. The gazebo from the 1893 Chicago World's Columbian Exposition is to the left of the house.

Perhaps the Wilson's vision for this residential development is best captured in the sales brochure circulated at the time to investors in particular. The Wilson's cottage was pictured on the first page, and their lush garden is featured as an indication of the richness of the land. Inside the original sales brochure in the Wilson's private collection the description of the tract stated:

OPPORTUNITY

This beautiful tract is on the extension of the North Park
Car Line running out Forthcamp Avenue, and is destined
to be one of the highest class residence districts around
our beautiful city.

It consists of about sixty acres of choice, rich land
that will grow any kind of fruits and flowers that may be
grown in a semitropical climate, as may be seen by a visit
to the grounds of the Wilson home, situated on the tract,
where may be seen growing in profusion the choicest vari-
eties of oranges, lemons, and beautiful flowers, that would
give one the impression that they had suddenly landed in
a tropical garden.

The tract before being subdivided was a fine orchard
and vineyard, and nearly all the lots are covered at the
present time with bearing fruit trees or vines.

A more ideal place for a cozy home would be hard to
find anywhere near Fresno. Every lot is high, sightly, and
commands a fine view of the snow-capped mountains in
the distance. Here the air is always pure, and breezes blow
during the hottest summer weather.

A good streetcar service is already maintained, the
cars passing directly through the center of the tract every
ten minutes, on the wide, beautiful boulevard known as
Wishon Avenue, which makes the most remote lots only
two blocks from the car line, and many can be purchased
if taken at once, that face directly on the boulevard.

Streetcars leaving the Southern Pacific Depot arrive
at the tract in ten minutes, and a fine double track road
in course of construction will give a quicker service to this
locality.

The building restrictions, while moderate, insure a high-class residence district, where none need be ashamed of his neighbor's house.

Many of our leading citizens have already secured residence sites in this beautiful tract, one investor being Mr. A. G. Wishon, the general manager of the Fresno Traction Company, who has purchased a full block, and the plans for a handsome residence are in the hands of his architect.

Fresno property, both city and country, is steadily advancing in price, and now is the time to get in on the ground floor, as only a limited number of lots will be sold at present prices.

Many of the wealthiest people in the world today have made their immense fortunes directly through buying real estate just outside of growing and progressive cities, and amassed wealth through the increased value of their holdings as these cities grew.

How many times have you said (and heard others say), "Why, a couple of years ago I could have bought such and such a piece of property for so and so much, and did not do it; just see what it is worth now."

Look around you in any high-class residence section of this city and see what property is selling for now, then ascertain what you could have purchased the same property for two or three years ago.

Look at the beautiful homes that have been built along Van Ness and Forthcamp Avenues in the last two years (and many now in course of construction), and see what you could have purchased lots for a short time ago, and at the same time ask what they are worth now.

Here is the whole thing in a nutshell. Buy property in a high-class residence district before prices advance, and you are bound to make money; wait until others have picked out the choicest lots and built homes and then you pay the other fellow the profit that might have been yours.

Don't put it off as you have done before; the property can never depreciate, it is bound to rise in value and make money while you sleep.

You can make more money by buying lots in the suburbs of a progressive city like Fresno, than by putting it in any savings bank in Christendom.

Remember those that are making the most money during these strenuous times are not the ones that work the hardest, but the ones who are investing their spare dollars in real estate in a flourishing community.

Buy real estate when cheap, and you are sure to more than double your money.

Now think of the opportunities you have let slip by, and make up your mind to have a home of your own, and pay rent to yourself, or if you already have a home, invest your savings in property that is bound to advance in value.

Call at our office and let us show you this property, and we feel assured that you will at once see the advantage of purchasing a few lots before prices advance.

It concludes with an assurance of sufficient infrastructure to support the homes and the geography to rise above the hoi polloi of the city: "The Wilson's North Fresno Tract has streets graded, sidewalks curbed, city water, low taxes, and high lots. In fact, the property is nine feet higher than Belmont Avenue."

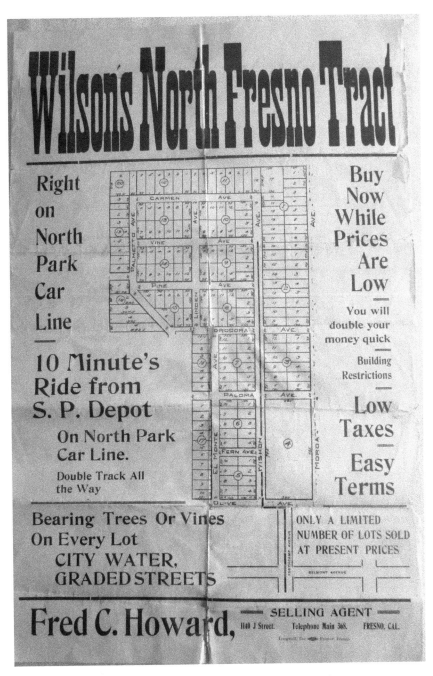

Original advertising poster for the Wilson's North Fresno Tract.

Lots began to sell immediately, slowly at first due in large part to World War I, then taking off in 1919 when the building boom began. Development continued for three decades. The Wilson Island portion of the tract in particular attracted, as intended, Fresno's wealthiest citizens, who often invested solely in lots they resold quickly at a profit. Others held onto the lots and built mansions or more modest homes designed by prominent architects of the day. The initial homeowners represent a who's who of Fresno at the turn of the twentieth century. Rosanna kept one house in the Wilson family for decades—the home at 1445 Echo Avenue—though she lived out her life at the family estate on the block at 831 Olive Avenue, on the northeast corner of Olive and Wishon. The Olive residence was torn down long ago after a fire demolished the third floor.

Her vision was ultimately fulfilled. The Wilson Island would become a registered historic district in 2009, arguably worthy of the recognition given to the homes and ranchos of Rosanna's ancestors that are today among California's historic landmarks. (See Appendix B.) Rosanna created a collection of period homes noted for their wide variety of architectural styles and representative of the developmental forces pushing the northern boundaries of Fresno in the early 1920s.

The Wilsons sold off the other portions of their land that stretched from the North Fresno Tract west all the way to Palm Avenue, presumably to subsidize either the initial development of Rosanna's tract or the investment in the Banana Plantation in Mexico that George was purchasing around this time. Within a few months of Rosanna filing her subdivision (November 1908), the Lucerne Tract subdivision was filed (1909). The four that followed mapped out residential neighborhoods reaching all the way over to Palm that are there today: the Earlhurst Tract (1910), the Maple Park Tract (1911), the Claremont Park Tract (1912), and the Allen and Binford Tract (1912). Street names changed as each tract connected to the previous ones, but one name is a clear reminder of the original owners. Notably, the street located halfway between Echo and Palm Avenues was initially named Central Avenue. However, by 1912, the name was changed to its current name, Wilson Avenue, in memory of the family that had owned the extensive ranch on which the homes were built. Lucerne Lane became Lucerne Avenue. McKinley, originally a north-south street just east of Palm, became Ferger. Echo Avenue has had three different names—Palmetto north of Floradora, Chester south of Floradora, and finally Echo once the two tracts connected. (See Appendix F.)

The odd angle at the intersection of Floradora and Echo on the original Wilsons' North Fresno Tract map, defining the southwest corner of the Wilson Island, suggests Rosanna had not yet made a decision about the configuration of the streets to the south and west. It was still all open space as far as the eye could see. The matter was actually resolved two years later when the Earlhurst Tract was surveyed. The north-south street that had been Palmetto to the north and Chester to the south of Floradora was straightened out (with just a slight jog still visible today) and given its current name, Echo Avenue. The change was completed before Rosanna sold the affected lots in her tract to buyers who began building in 1920.

Based on the sequencing of the sale of subdivisions to the west between 1908 and 1912, it is safe to conclude that a critical part of the overarching vision of both Rosanna and George was to use a portion of their initial investment to generate a cash flow to support other ventures. Rosanna had seen how the Coopers in particular had used land to expand their empire. She understood how effective use of land could sustain long-term profits. She learned when to take risks, supported in the initial years by her husband the quintessential adventurer at her side. Although she had lost her husband and was estranged from the Coopers at the time of burgeoning development of her land, she demonstrated for the remainder of her life that she was more than capable of building and leading a multi-million-dollar empire.

CHAPTER 5

CONSTRUCTION BEGINS, 1910

When Rosanna Wilson filed her tract map in 1908, her plan included what has become the Wilson Island Historic District. Seventy-eight homes contribute to the district. Only two of the eighty in this neighborhood do not meet the requirement for historic recognition that the home be constructed prior to 1970. The district, virtually complete by the 1930s, is a visual time capsule of upscale residences in early Fresno, when people who worked downtown walked, took the streetcar, drove a buggy, or in some cases drove a car. The homes appeared gradually over a period of three decades between 1910 and 1939 that spanned three distinct periods in our nation's history: World War I, the Roaring Twenties, and the Great Depression of the 1930s, corresponding respectively to a slow building start in the Wilson Island, followed by a building boom beginning in 1919, and ending with gradual infill through the 1930s.

The Mosgrove Home, the first house built in the Wilson Island, 1910.

William Mosgrove, a local realtor, was the first to build his home at 660 East Pine Avenue in 1910, the same year Fresno City College was established downtown on O Street. From their house on the corner of Pine and Linden near the southern edge of the future historic district, his son recalled being able to see all the way to the tops of the trees near what he thought was the San Joaquin River. Public building records are absent for the other early builders. However, a contemporaneous newspaper article and the 1919 Sanborn provide clues to their construction dates. For example, in 1915, the Fresno newspaper announced the completion of the William and Bessie Parlier home at 667 East Home Avenue.

667 E. Home Avenue. The Parlier Home

"Fresno – 1916 – east of drill tower on S. P. railroad reservation." Vandor 1919

Specific construction dates for the other ten earliest homes can be estimated based on the 1919 Sanborn map of Fresno. Only one house was constructed in 1918, and it did not appear on the 1919 Sanborn map, suggesting that if a home appeared on the 1919 map it had to have been completed prior to 1918. Thus, one might conclude that these earliest ten homes—primarily in the southern half of the Wilson Island—were built sometime between 1910 and 1917, as the nation's attention and resources turned to preparations for war, and during the time when the 1916 Historic Old Administration Building of Fresno City College was built. (See Table 1.)

Table 1. Homes on the Sanborn map, likely built 1910-1917				
Street	**#**	**Name of Home**	**Built**	**Architecture**
E. Carmen	701	The Mary S. Wallace Home	pre-1919	Airplane bungalow
E. Home	655	The Ivan C. & Maude McIndoo Home	pre-1919	Prairie-Craftsman
	667	The William & Bessie Parlier Home	1915	Airplane bungalow with Japanese roof treatment; referenced in McAlester's Museum Homes, p 48
E. Pine	660	The Mosgrove Home	1910	Craftsman bungalow (Frank Faulkner); individual Historic Property #106
	701	The Berton & Edna R. Einstein Home	pre-1919	Italian Renaissance revival
	711	The Minnie Sachs Home	pre-1919	Italian Renaissance inspired with Prairie and Craftsman influences
	727	The Mary Cohen Home	pre-1919	highly altered Craftsman bungalow, enlarged in 1952
	748-54	The Wishon-Pine Apartments	pre-1919	former Prairie style moved from front to rear lot to add commercial portion
E. Floradora	707	The Frank Curtain Home	1912	Craftsman style
	717	The L. Samuels Home	pre-1919	Prairie box with Craftsman and Colonial Revival details
	743	The Henry Gundelfinger Home	pre-1919	Prairie box variation
N. Echo	1497	The Luther S. Brown Home	pre-1919	Bungalow

701 E. Carmen Avenue. The Mary S. Wallace Home

655 E. Home Avenue. The Ivan C. and Maude McIndoo Home

701 E. Pine Avenue. The Berton and Edna R. Einstein Home

711 E. Pine Avenue. The Minnie Sachs Home

727 E. Pine Avenue. The Mary Cohen Home

748-754 E. Pine Avenue. The Wishon Pine Apartments

707 E. Floradora Avenue. The Frank Curtain Home

717 E. Floradora Avenue. The L. Samuels Home

743 E. Floradora Avenue. The Gundelfinger Home

1497 N. Echo Avenue. The Luther S. Brown Home

In addition to the impact of war efforts, other investments that Rosanna and George managed vied for her attention. Between 1905 and 1911, their controlling interest in the banana plantation near Puerta Vallarta, Mexico, pulled them away from Fresno. Rosanna often traveled there with George, usually in January to oversee preparations for production and importing. Closer to home, she bought a lot in Santa Cruz in 1904 and in 1911 applied for a building permit to construct what would become their summer cottage. And George, the person she relied on initially to negotiate the construction of the streetcar line from downtown to the Wilson's North Fresno Tract, was increasingly in ill health. Nonetheless, he too was actively looking for land investments outside of Fresno, as evidenced by his letter in the Wilson's private collection to the David Jacks Corporation in 1913 expressing his desire to purchase one thousand acres of their land " . . . on the southeast of the county road probably six or seven miles from Monterey." Unfortunately, his passing in 1915 ended negotiations over potential additional land purchases. Thus, between the impact of national war efforts and Rosanna's personal circumstances, it is not surprising that construction in the Wilson Island slowed for eight years.

With the war drawing to a close, Rosanna needed to find a way to renew land sales and construction. So in 1918, under her direction, her son, AP, obtained a building permit for the only home to be built that year (at 625 East Home).[31]

625 E. Home Avenue. The Charles T. and Rhoda J. Cearly Home

It drew community attention back to her investment that resulted in an unparalleled boom in 1919 when twelve homes were constructed in a single year, almost half of them on Carmen Avenue at the northern edge of the Wilson Island. But the 1918 house was not the only thing working in her favor. Though the area felt like the northern extremity of Fresno back in 1908 when Rosanna first filed the tract map, her tract was now prime real estate for another reason. In 1919, Fresno architects Coates and Traver designed three Classical buildings for the new location of Fresno High across McKinley on North Echo Avenue just a block north of Rosanna's land. Classes moved from the old, overcrowded location on O Street downtown in fall 1921, and the school was dedicated on February 18, 1922. Streetcar lines that opened between 1912 and 1914 facilitated the commute to downtown when they connected affluent residents to the business district.

Construction in the Wilson Island was robust through most of the 1920s, with 63 percent of the homes completed by the end of that decade before the Great Depression. The remainder were completed primarily in the late 1930s toward the end of the Great Depression, and a few as late as the 1940s. Despite the poor economy in the Depression years, twenty-two new homes were added in that decade by some of the most prominent Fresnans of the time, creating jobs for at least a small number of the many unemployed of the decade. (See Figures 1 and 2.)

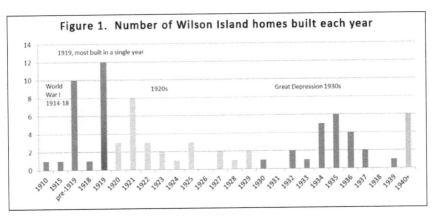

Figure 1. Number of Wilson Island homes built each year

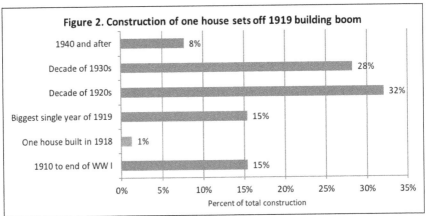

Figure 2. Construction of one house sets off 1919 building boom

As the lots were being sold to investors, developers, architects, and future homeowners, Rosanna and AP personally oversaw the construction of eight homes. Allegedly, in an effort to make the homes attractive to exclusive buyers, they imported chandeliers from Europe and added other special features. Perhaps her four-month grand tour of Europe in 1930 was, if not in part a business excursion, at least an opportunity to gather new ideas for architectural designs and features for inclusion in the last few homes to be built. With the exception of the one house built in 1918 to kick off postwar construction, the mother-son Wilson team obtained most of the building permits in a three-year period between 1919 and 1921, primarily for lots along Echo Avenue. In addition, Rosanna retained three lots on Echo Avenue for a long time, selling them much later in the 1930s. (See Table 2.)

Table 2. Lots retained and/or developed by Rosanna, AP, or Delfina			
Street	**Number**	**Date built**	**AP or Rosanna Wilson, or Delfina Cooper**
N. Echo	1445	1921	Building permit issued to AP; home retained by Rosanna C Wilson and descendants until 1948
	1455	1921	Building permit issued to AP
	1475	1935	Rosanna C Wilson retained the lot
	1485	1920	Building permit issued to AP
	1487	1920	Building permit issued to AP
	1515	1937	Rosanna C Wilson retained the lot
	1525	1934	Rosanna C Wilson retained the lot
E. Carmen	600	1919	Building permit issued to AP
	630	1920	Building permit issued to AP
E. Home	625	1918	Building permit issued to AP
	630	1919	Building permit issued to AP
	659	1954	AP and his wife turned the lot over to Delfina Cooper in December 1916; she sold it to McIndoo in 1923; left vacant until building permit issued to Sadoyan in 1954

One house on Echo Avenue merits special mention, the large home at 1445 that defines the southwest corner of the Wilson Island. In the original plan, the lot was quite a bit bigger than it is today, primarily because the streets in that corner were not yet in their final configuration. Adjacent tracts had not been surveyed. When she filed her original subdivision map in 1908, Rosanna had not yet figured out how the Wilson's North Fresno Tract would line up with the next ones to the south and west. So, she simply made a closed loop where Floradora met Palmetto (now Echo). If that had not changed, the front yard at 1445 N Echo Avenue would have been expansive, extending halfway into the facing block on Floradora (to about 653 Floradora). (See Appendix D for street configuration on original tract map and F for street name changes.) It was resolved when the next tracts to the south and west, Lucerne and Earlhurst, were surveyed in 1909 and 1910 respectively. The street Rosanna had named Palmetto, and called Chester in the Earlhurst Tract, finally became today's Echo when the two streets were aligned. Still visible today is a slight jog at the intersection of Echo and Floradora, a subtle reminder of the merger.

1445 N. Echo Avenue. The Rosanna C. Wilson Home

The house at 1445 Echo was constructed under the oversight of her son, whose signature was discovered in 2017 under original wallpaper. In 1921, she turned the lot over to AP, who then secured the building permit for a garage and a home designed by Shorb and Meade at an estimated construction cost of $18,000 (equivalent to about $235,000 in 2018). Upon its completion in 1922, the house reverted to Rosanna, who kept it in her family for the next twenty-six years. Rosanna never lived in the house, as she remained her entire life in the family mansion on the block at Olive and Wishon. According to her granddaughter, the home on Echo was an investment she originally intended to sell soon after it was built, but when she could not get the desired price in a depressed economy, she kept it instead and rented it out. She did own some of the contents (notably the silverware) which, upon her death, were distributed to her daughter and grandchildren along with ownership of the house. In February 1948, seven months after she died, the house was sold for the first time, marking the end of her involvement in the Wilson Island.

The Wilson Island is a step back into turn-of-the-twentieth-century Fresno opulence in architecture recognized for its historic value since at least 1985. Seven of the homes are considered museum-quality structures by the McAlesters in their *Field Guide to America's Historic Neighborhoods and Museum Houses in the Western States* (1998).[32] Three years of intensive research and travel resulted in their selection of a limited number of homes in intact neighborhoods across the country that would be of interest to visitors from elsewhere. Prominent Fresno architects such as Shorb and Meade, and Taylor-Wheeler designed a number of Wilson Island homes. And, as of this writing, seven homes are individually listed on the local Fresno Historic Register, noted for their architecture as well as the prominence of their early owners. (See Table 3.)

Table 3. Individually listed historic properties				
Street	**#**	**Home Name**	**Built**	**Architecture & individual listing #**
E. Carmen	660	The Deacon-Eilert Home	1919	Tudor/Craftsman; individual Historic Property #266
	718	The Dudley & Elsie Bates Home	1925	Prairie style; individual Historic Property #294
E. Home	625	The Cearly-Twining Home	1918	grand Period Revival; individual Historic Property #244
E. Pine	601	The Nis Johnson Home	1921	the only Mission Revival; individual Historic Property #245
	617	The Gustav & Edith Manheim Home	1919	Prairie with neoclassical proportions & massing; individual Historic Property #258
	640	The Gates-Twining Home	1932	only French Norman Revival (Taylor-Wheeler); individual Historic Property #239
	660	The Mosgrove Home	1910	Craftsman bungalow (Frank Faulkner); individual Historic Property #106

Fireplaces in at least five homes were made of tiles designed by the famous tile-maker of the Arts and Crafts period, Ernest Batchelder, whose innovative work was much sought after in his lifetime and is now highly prized. These homes are included in the inventory of Batchelder fireplaces maintained by the Pasadena Museum of History. (See Table 4.)

Table 4. Homes in the Wilson Island with Batchelder tile fireplaces		
Historic home	**Date built**	**Address**
The Deacon-Eilert Home	1919	660 E. Carmen Ave
The George Riddell Miller Home	1919	617 E. Carmen Ave
The Mary S. Wallace Home	Prior to 1919	701 E. Carmen Ave
The William & Anna Bean Home	1921	654 E. Home Ave
The W. Wacasar Home	1929	639 E. Floradora Ave

601 E. Pine. The Nis Johnson Home

617 E. Pine. The Gustav and Edith Manheim Home

Wilson Island homes were featured in the La Paloma Guild's Tenth Annual Heritage Home Tour in 1985. And showcased again in 1990 in "A Guide to Historic Architecture: Tower District," prepared by Russell C. Fey. The brochure for the self-guided tour described the architectural styles of virtually all the historic homes and commented that: "Instead of a single style, many buildings were constructed with a combination of styles. For example, a Georgian doorway might be applied to a Classical Revival home. A bungalow might be given an English or French flavor. Often a Monterey balcony was added to a Spanish Revival home. As a result, the character of the neighborhood is radically different from the contemporary subdivisions of today."

In 2005, the Fresno Historical Society highlighted ten homes in its "Fresno's Wilson Island Historic Home Tour." That same summer, their publication, "The Grapevine," included the residential area in a headline story.

In short, Rosanna created a virtual outdoor museum. As a result of the Tower District Specific Plan (March 26, 1991), it benefits from municipal guidelines and resources designed to preserve the historic, distinctive character of what was a gateway to downtown Fresno to the south and a vibrant residential expansion to the north. As mentioned in the plan, preservation of neighborhoods like this is " . . . an essential component to the community development process for achieving stability and retaining quality in areas such as the Tower District" (Tower District Specific Plan 1991). Rosanna's legacy to Fresno has had an impact far beyond what she may have imagined in 1908 when she filed her plan to subdivide sixty acres of her land.

CHAPTER 6

A WHO'S WHO OF FRESNO:
WHO BOUGHT INTO THE NEIGHBORHOOD
IN THE EARLY YEARS?

They were Fresno's business leaders, entrepreneurs and investors, bankers and judges. They were the founders of commercial enterprises whose impact was felt throughout the Central Valley and, in some cases, beyond. A few were descendants or close friends of the city's founding fathers. With offices downtown in the old heart of Fresno and homes often within a few blocks on nearby residential streets, they were looking to move away from the growing din of downtown as business expanded. Wives created the social fabric of the community through their myriad clubs, while their husbands expanded their connections through memberships in various fraternal organizations from the local Elks, Masons, and Rotary to San Francisco's Bohemian Club. One can only speculate about what attracted them to the new neighborhood. Exclusivity and investment potential were two possible incentives. The Wilson Island was on the leading edge of northern residential expansion where the well-to-do could separate themselves from average citizens. It offered the opportunity to build a dream home with a large yard, or profit from the resale of highly desirable lots. Their stays in the Wilson Island ranged from barely a year to a few decades. In some cases, it was a fleeting investment intended to turn a quick profit on a home they probably never lived in themselves.

Rosanna subdivided her land at the northern end of her tract, in what would become known today as the Wilson Island, into eighty-five lots measuring 75 feet wide by 150 feet deep.[33] The initial sales marked the beginning of three decades of negotiations with buyers over lot size and the specifications of the house they would build. Regardless of whether the home was a mansion three or four times the size of a typical house of that era equipped with a card and billiard room, or something more modest, the buyers over the next thirty years collectively established the persona of the neighborhood that set it apart. The following are but a few examples of the people who bought in.

SPECULATORS

The earliest investor was the realtor William Mosgrove, who also became a longtime resident. He owned at least three lots in the Wilson Island, the first one purchased in 1910 for his own home built at 660 Pine, and two lots purchased nine years later as investments with his real estate partner, Frank L. Petty. The Pine residence remained in his family for over sixty years until 1973. However, the development and resale of one of his other lots is representative of the actions of numerous speculators who would buy a lot, build the home, and quickly sell it for a profit during the Wilson Island building boom that began in 1919. The lot is at 730 Pine one block east of his home.[34]

730 E. Pine Avenue. The Harry and Lucille Mitchell Home

The house he and Petty had constructed on it changed owners twice within about thirty months before finding a more permanent resident. Immediately after its completion, Fresno's former Mayor W. Parker Lyon purchased the house, only to sell it within a year to Lester H. Eastin. The thirty-five-year-old Eastin was already a very prominent businessman in Fresno as the manager and part owner of the Roeding Fig and Olive Company. Their business extended to Europe and all parts of the United States. Notably, the first shipment of figs from California consisted of five tons packed at the Fresno ranch of George C. Roeding (Vandor 1919). But Eastin did not keep the house long either. Within sixteen months, he sold it to the Harry C. Mitchell family, who lived there for the next fifty years.

It's not clear if Eastin ever resided in the Wilson Island, as he is associated with multiple addresses. Perhaps they were merely temporary investments. In voter registration and city directories for the same year, he reported his residence address both as 730 Pine and 654 Home (though he was never the registered owner of the latter). He did purchase another house at 727 Pine a few years later, but again held it for only a few months before selling. Multiple turnovers in a short span of time suggest they were either investments or he was a very mobile homeowner.

654 E. Home Avenue. The William and Anna Bean Home

NOB HILL RESIDENTS INVEST EARLY

In the 1880s, the area around Tulare and K Streets (now Van Ness), referred to as "Nob Hill," was home to some of Fresno's founding fathers, including the Gundelfingers, Einsteins, and Rowells.[35] Expansion of the business district south past Tulare Avenue encroached on Nob Hill around the same time that the emergence of choice residential areas north of downtown drew a few of their descendants and close friends to the Wilson Island. In an era when merchants were the bankers, Louis Einstein and the three Gundelfinger brothers were one of two leading Fresno mercantile groups, the other being the Kutner-Goldstein group. They were rivals in every respect, personally and professionally, for forty years before they both expanded the competition by creating their own banks. The Einstein-Gundelfinger group formed the Fresno-based Bank of Central California in 1887 to compete with the Kutner-Goldstein group's Farmers Bank of Fresno, formed in 1882 with ties to San Francisco (Walker 1941). Members of the Einstein and Gundelfinger families moved to the Wilson Island. Kutners and Goldsteins did not. One of the earliest homes (at 743 Floradora) was built by Henry Gundelfinger, a stockholder in the Bank of Central California.

743 E. Floradora. The Henry Gundelfinger Home

Berton and Edna Einstein were also among the early arrivals to the Wilson Island. Berton had grown up in the family home on K Street downtown in the late 1800s, where the Gundelfingers and Rowells were neighbors on the same street. In his early thirties, around the time they built their home at 701 Pine, he had followed in his father's footsteps and was a bank president considered a rising magnate. They remained on Pine for about ten years until they sold the home to Chase Osborn, newspaper owner.

701 E. Pine Avenue. The Berton and Edna R. Einstein Home

710 E. Pine Avenue. The Lee and Minita Blasingame Home

Within several years of the Gundelfingers and Einsteins building their homes, Milo L. Rowell bought in with the purchase in 1923 of the completed home at 710 Pine from well-known financier Lee A. Blasingame, who'd had it built in 1919. Like Lester Eastin, Rowell and Blasingame were more likely investors with little intention of residing in the home for any length of time or at all, as in Rowell's case. Rowell remained at his longtime residence at 1037 U Street downtown during the brief period he owned the home on Pine. According to the local newspaper, he undoubtedly had money to invest in a new venture, if that is indeed what he was doing. In the midst of a family crisis three years earlier, when his fourteen-year-old son was kidnapped for ransom, the newspaper referred to Milo as " . . . the millionaire resident of Fresno, and nephew of Chester H. Rowell, member of the US Shipping Board. . . . " (and California senator for ten years). Milo was trustee of Sun-Maid Raisins and continued a lengthy career in agricultural production. For thirty years, between 1900 and 1930, he was the manager of Hobbs-Parsons Produce Company of which he ultimately became the principal owner, credited with developing and expanding the company into the largest produce firm in the San Joaquin Valley (Walker 1946, Walker 1941). He influenced development of the area downtown on Van Ness Avenue from Inyo to Mariposa including land along Tulare. He built the Hotel Virginia and was the major owner and manager of the Rowell Building. In short, he was an investor. He held onto the property on Pine for three years before selling it to H. J. and Grace Craycroft, who remained there for nine years.

Lee A. Blasingame had enlisted architects Shorb and Meade to design the Craycrofts' house in 1919. Blasingame was a member of a very prosperous and well-known ranching family with a home base in the foothills. His career had taken many turns, as was typical of the times. He was a native son born in 1861 on Dry Creek Ranch in Fresno County. After college, he began his business experience as a bookkeeper, and later cashier, for the First National Bank in Fresno. In that era, the cashier effectively managed the bank, which afforded him the opportunity to establish a valuable network of contacts that undoubtedly gave him insight into potential investments, the Wilson Island among them. Upon leaving the bank, he joined his brother, Alfred Blasingame, in farming and stock raising, especially sheep and cattle, at their headquarters at the Blasingame Ranch. He was a member of the Bohemian Club in San Francisco with interests in viticulture. On his 145-acre vineyard seven miles northeast of Fresno (at about the location of Gettysburg and Winery Avenues today), he used the most up-to-date equipment for developing specimen plants (Vandor 1919). But it was his pastime that featured him in the news—the winning silks of his racehorses!

If Blasingame actually lived in the house, it was not for more than one or two years, as his primary business interests appear to have been elsewhere. Piecing together census and voter registration records, he gave his home address as 710 Pine only once, in 1922. From 1916 to 1934, he voted consistently in the Sierra Precinct (which included Clovis), and for decades he used PO Box 790 in Fresno while operating out of the ranch in the foothills. His reasons for building the house on Pine are lost to history. While owning the house as a short-term investment, he may have occupied it as a townhouse.

The Bankers and Businessmen Who Stayed

Another Blasingame did take up residence in the Wilson Island. William O. Blasingame was thirteen years younger than his brother Lee and a banker rather than a stockman like his father and other brothers (Vandor 1919). It was William who had visited George Wilson at the Chicago World's Columbian Exposition back in 1893. William and

Edna bought a double lot at 630 Carmen from Rosanna Wilson in 1920. Her son, AP, obtained the building permit for him and oversaw construction of the house designed by Shorb and Meade. The Blasingames remained there for the next fourteen years but lost the house during the Depression. Neighborhood lore says it became a boarding house prior to its sale in 1934 to Archibald B. MacAlpine, manager of the Fresno Brewing Company on M Street, whose family lived there for the next thirteen years.

630 E. Carmen Avenue. The William O. and Edna Blasingame Home

At the same time Rosanna was negotiating the sale with W. O. Blasingame, she was also negotiating the sale of the property next door to the east with Roual Deacon, owner of a Lemoore-based lumber company, who was constructing a house for William J. and Mae Eilert at 660 Carmen. Notes on the original deed indicate that Deacon and Eilert wanted a double lot as well, but Blasingame got there first. Although they were not able to procure the entire desired portion of the lot to the west, Deacon and Eilert ended up with something close—property just twenty-five feet short of being a double lot.

660 E. Carmen Avenue. The Deacon-Eilert Home

Eilert was well known in the business community as the cofounder (with his father) and owner of the Fresno Brewing Company at the foot of M Street downtown (listed today individually on the local historic register).[36] Eilert and W. O. Blasingame, next-door neighbors in the Wilson Island, knew each other well through their bank dealings. In 1925, they were both members of the Executive Board of the Fidelity of Fresno Branch, Pacific Southwest Trust and Savings Bank. By the time Deacon[37] turned the new home over to the Eilerts, Prohibition was well underway. Known statewide as an activist supporting the production and consumption of alcohol, Eilert had to have found the impact of Prohibition to be a challenge. To this day, his house is rumored to have been a hub of bootlegging activity. In Eilert's retirement years, *Fresno Bee* society columns occasionally mentioned him as an avid sportsman with summer homes at Shaver and Bass Lakes. He died in 1934, one year after Prohibition ended and the same year the manager of his revived brewery, MacAlpine, moved in next door following the departure of the Blasingames. Mae Eilert remained in the Carmen Avenue home for another eleven years. Thus, for its first two decades, the 660 Carmen Avenue residence was occupied by only two people and an occasional guest.

1445 N. Echo Avenue. The Rosanna C. Wilson Home

1455 N. Echo Avenue. The Lena A. Shaver Home

Eilert also crossed paths with a fellow sportsman from Michigan, Charles B. Shaver, who helped develop the reservoir known as Shaver Lake and who built the lumber flume that terminated at Clovis. Shaver's widow, Lena, bought the lot at 1455 Echo next door to Rosanna Wilson's at 1445. Lena Shaver was a business force in her own right who had erected a then-modern building on the southwest corner of Merced and Fulton Streets downtown after her husband's death in 1907 (Walker 1941). Together with AP Wilson, she obtained the building permit for the home on Echo Avenue in 1920, around the same time Blasingame and Eilert were buying lots and building their homes in the neighborhood. Her home on Echo would remain in the Shaver family for almost four decades.

630 E. Home Avenue. The Frank and Margaret Bradford Home

Among the prominent businessmen and long-term residents was commercial entrepreneur Frank Bradford. He was owner of the San Joaquin Baking Company, the largest in the Central Valley, and like many of his colleagues a community leader (Walker 1941). Bradford erected his plant at the corner of L and Los Angeles Streets in 1918 and the following year bought the lot at 630 Home, where he built the home that stayed in the Bradford family for thirty-five years and is still connected to their descendants.

Finally, a later arrival indicative of the prominence of the businessmen who continued to seek homes in this neighborhood was Frank W. Twining, the son and business partner of well-known Dr. Frank E. Twining, founder and owner of Twining Laboratories, established in 1898. It quickly became one of the most important scientific testing labs in the state, a reputation it still enjoys today (Walker 1941). Arriving in 1936, Frank W. Twining is representative of the second wave of buyers. His home was at 640 Pine Avenue.

Top: 640 E. Pine Avenue. The Gates-Twining Home, 2018
Bottom: The Gates-Twining Home in the 1930s.

THE ATTORNEYS AND JUDGES

Frank Curtain was an early arrival to the Wilson Island at 707 Flordadora in 1913. The Curtains bought the house from Robert Barton who built it in about 1912. At the time Frank was a successful attorney in Fresno who was preparing to run for district attorney in 1914. Surviving photos of the house at the time confirm the remoteness of the neighborhood and the sparse landscapes in those early days. The house would remain in the Curtain family for the next ninety-five years, until it was finally sold in 2008, the longest documented period of ownership of any house in the Wilson Island.

707 E. Floradora Avenue. The Frank Curtain Home

The Frank Curtain family on the front porch of their home at 707 E. Floradora Avenue.

Visible in the distance on the left is the Mosgrove home on Pine Avenue.

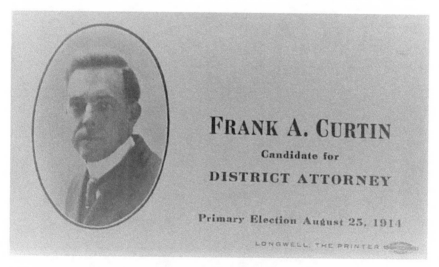

Frank Curtain's card when he ran for district attorney in Fresno, 1914.

Joining the Curtains and their business and commercial colleagues in the neighborhood in the 1920s and 1930s were no less than five notable members of Fresno's legal community, four of whom built their own homes.

605 E. Carmen Avenue. The Bingham-Lovejoy Home

The only one who did not was George R. Lovejoy, who, in 1926, acquired the house at 605 Carmen Avenue built by realtors William Mosgrove and Frank Perry. It was a short commute to his office at the time in the Brix Building downtown. Lovejoy was the Fresno district attorney whose decision in 1933 made the newspaper: "Realizing that it is becoming more and more difficult to obtain convictions upon the testimony of 'stool pigeons,' district Attorney George R. Lovejoy announced he will permanently abandon the system. He said he will hire private detectives or other investigators upon a salary or per diem basis to carry on the work formerly done by 'stool pigeons.'" (*The Fresno Bee/The Fresno Republican* June 23, 1933).

The four who did build their own homes were Thomas R. Thomson (1545 Echo Avenue in 1926), Frank Kauke (641 Carmen Avenue in 1931), Philip Conley (718 Carmen Avenue in 1932), and Claude Rowe (631 Carmen Ave in 1933).

1545 N. Echo Avenue. The Thomas and Ada Mae Thomson Home

Perhaps best known among them was Judge Thomas R. Thomson, who had a statewide reputation as a jurist frequently called to hear important cases in other counties. He was president of the Fresno Bar Association in 1923 and US Bankruptcy Referee from 1924 to 1928. In 1926, he and his wife, Ada Mae, had their home built on the lot at 1545 Echo Avenue. Soon thereafter, in 1929, he was appointed to the Superior Court Bench of Fresno County by Governor C. C. Young to fill a vacancy. The following year, he was elected for a six-year term and reelected two more times, holding the position for eighteen years. His legal career included many accomplishments. For example, he successfully sponsored and drafted the Constitutional Amendment authorizing the legislature to create the Fourth Appellate Court to sit in Fresno (Walker 1946).

641 E. Carmen Avenue. The Frank and Felita Kauke Home

The Frank and Felita Kauke home at 641 Carmen Avenue had a sad beginning. Attorney Frank Kauke bought the lot in 1931 from fellow attorney Irvin Aten with the intention of building a home as a wedding gift for his new bride, Felita. That year, he applied for a building permit for a structure with an estimated construction cost of $10,857. Sadly, he died four years later in 1935, but Felita never left her husband's wedding gift, where she remained for the next thirty-three years until she passed away.

718 E. Carmen Avenue. The Dudley and Elsie Bates Home

A block east on Carmen, Philip Conley arrived at 718 Carmen in 1932. Conley was the native son of then-well-known Judge W. Conley of Madera. When Madera was organized, his father was the first Superior Court Judge elected, and the youngest in the state at age twenty-six. He held the office for twenty-eight years, resigning in 1921 to take up practice with his sons, Philip and Matthew, in Fresno. When he moved to the Wilson Island about ten years later, Philip was a well-established attorney in Fresno (Walker 1946). Philip's career included serving as deputy district attorney in 1921–22, judge of the Fresno County Superior Court, and the first presiding judge of the California Court of Appeal, fifth Appellate District in Fresno.

631 E. Carmen Avenue. The Claude and Laura Rowe Home

The fourth attorney joined the neighborhood in 1933, next door to the Kaukes. Claude Loftus Rowe, an alumnus of the University of California (as were many of his colleagues), was relatively new to the profession when at the age of thirty-three, he had his home built on the lot at 631 Carmen Avenue. The house was handed down to his son and remained in the Rowe family for the next forty-five years.

REALTORS, INSURANCE BROKERS, AND NEWSPAPER MOGULS

In a few cases, multiple members of the same family bought homes in the Wilson Island. The best example was the Levy brothers, prominent real estate and insurance businessmen who moved into the neighborhood between 1922 and 1934. Ben, Herbert, and Sigmund bought vacant lots and built homes at 641 Pine (1922), 666 Home (1930), and 1549 Echo (1934), respectively. Herbert, the eldest, worked for ten years at the Farmers

National Bank in Fresno before deciding to strike out in his own business. He and his brother Leon formed the Levy Brothers real estate and insurance firm. Herbert was a leader in the industry who became president of the Realty Board in 1924, prior to building his home in 1930. He was the second Levy brother to move into the Wilson Island.

641 E. Pine Avenue. The Benjamin Levy Home

666 E. Home Avenue. The Herbert Levy Home

1549 N. Echo Avenue. The Sigmund Levy Home

His youngest brother, Ben, was the first in 1922 at age thirty with his wife, Leah, and their young children. Ben's small, one-story house stood in contrast to the two-story built eight years later at almost twice the construction cost by his older brother Herbert a block away on Home. Ben had joined the firm in 1913. He remained at that house for fifteen years until 1937, three years after their third brother moved here.

Finally, in 1934, their oldest brother, Sigmund, moved to Echo Avenue. He was also the last to join the firm (in 1917) that Herbert had started. Sigmund had a career in the newspaper business. He began as a reporter on the editorial staff of the *Fresno Tribune*. At the *Fresno Morning Republican*, he rose to become advertising manager. Sigmund was active in civic affairs and had been connected to the Raisin Festival since its inception (Winchell 1933). His home remained in the Levy family for fifty-two years and sold for the first time in 1986. The Herbert Levy home is the only one that remains in the family as of this writing.

605 E. Home. The George and Emma Osborn Home

Sigmund was not the only neighbor with a media career. The brothers George A. and Chase S. Osborn bought lots at 605 Home and 701 Pine respectively. In October 1920, Chester Rowell sold the *Fresno Morning Republican* to the brothers, sons of the former Governor C. S. Osborn of Michigan, for around a million dollars. For the previous three years, the Osborn brothers had been publishing the *Fresno Herald* and continued to operate both papers for three years until they were merged (Walker 1941). George purchased the Wilson Island lot and built his house at 605 Home within a year of purchasing the newspaper from Rowell. His brother Chase may have intended to follow George into the Wilson Island when he purchased the lot at 701 Pine in 1926 from the Berton Einsteins, but although he held onto it for ten years, he never did build a home there.

THE ARCHITECTS AND BUILDERS

Dennis B. Wheeler was best known as a founding partner with Orville R. Taylor of Taylor-Wheeler, the firm that developed the five-acre Terrace Gardens residential area on Terrace between Wilson and Palm north of Clinton around 1930. Taylor was the designer, and Wheeler was the superintendent of construction. Their firm also designed and constructed several Wilson Island homes, as well as remodels and additions to existing homes. Wheeler was at the beginning of his career when, in 1927, he built his modest home with a garage at 661 Floradora for an estimated construction cost of $3,500. He lived there for the next eight years, though his influence on construction in the neighborhood was felt for many years thereafter.

661 E. Floradora. The Dennis B. Wheeler Home

Well-known architect Richard Felchlin arrived in the Wilson Island in the mid-1930s during the Great Depression. His well-known and successful firm designed, engineered, and constructed the Pacific Southwest Building that opened in 1925. At the time, his office was nearby in the Bank of Italy Building downtown. Later, he became president of the Grant-Pacific Rock Company and eventually built his home at 665 Carmen in 1935, where he remained until his death in 1960.

665 E. Carmen Avenue. The Richard F. Felchlin Home

600 E. Carmen Avenue. The Claude M. Thompson Home

Before he moved in, Felchlin was quite familiar with another resident across the street at the other end of the block, Claude Thompson (at 600 Carmen). The Thompson Brothers Company was actively engaged in numerous street improvements around Fresno in 1920 as the city's travel arteries were paved, and sidewalks and gutters added. Examples of a few of his projects include nearby Vassar Avenue between Maroa and Wishon, Whitebridge Avenue then at the western edge of the city, the extension of Elm Street to the south, and 5.35 miles of paving up Blackstone Avenue. The Thompson Brothers Company had done all the excavation work on the Pacific Southwest building that Felchlin had designed, and they supplied all the rock and sand. It was a massive project. With a footprint of eighty by one hundred feet, the construction cost of the twelve-story building was estimated at $1,000,000. Claude had been living in the Wilson Island since 1923 before the new building opened, having bought the home designed by Shorb and Meade under contract to AP Wilson back in 1919. The Felchlins and Thompsons were social friends as well as business colleagues. Their wives had been members of the same bridge club that met occasionally at the home of another acquaintance on Echo, well before Felchlin decided to purchase the lot on Carmen.

731 E. Carmen Avenue. The Harrison B. and Nancy Traver Home

Harrison Traver, a fellow well-known architect of the era, had been living in the next block east of Felchlin's lot since 1919, at 731 Carmen, where he and his wife built their home. He is best known for his work with W.D. Coates, designing Fresno, Porterville, and Hanford High Schools, and the A.G. Wishon mansion. Upon the completion of Porterville High School in 1923, the *Los Angeles Times* noted it as among the best in the state. Coates & Traver and the Richard Felchlin Company also had neighboring offices on the sixth floor of the Rowell Building at the peak of their careers.

Traver was the first architect to join the Wilson Island and overlapped with the Thompsons for five years. By the time the Felchlins moved in, Traver had left and the Thompsons would remain for only two more years. Nonetheless, they collectively reflect the influx of numerous members of the building and construction community who established their homes in the neighborhood over the years—owners of planing mills and lumber companies as well as architects and engineers who saw this as a desirable, up-and-coming residential area.

DESCENDANTS MOVE IN

The generations of homeowners naturally turned over. As often happened then and now in the Wilson Island, children inherited the homes or in some cases bought homes of their own in the Wilson Island. The Mosgroves, the very first residents, are but one example. Their daughter, Lois, and son-in-law, Edwin R. Scarboro, MD, were part of the second wave when in 1936 they moved into 627 Pine, a few doors west of the home she grew up in. Their house, now known as the Gerald and Margherita Thomas Home, was named after Lois's grandparents, who built it in 1919. The Scarboros lived there for the next fourteen years. Dr. Scarboro was president of the Fresno County Medical Society in 1932 and resident physician at the General Hospital where he was in charge of neurology cases (Walker 1946). Altogether, multiple generations of the Mosgrove family lived in the Wilson Island for over sixty years, from 1910 to 1973.

627 E. Pine Avenue. The Gerald and Margherita Thomas Home

Two families retained their homes longer through successive generations: the Curtains at 707 Floradora (for ninety-five years from 1913 to 2008) and the Herbert Levy family at 666 Home. The Levy home has been handed down in the family since 1930, when it was first constructed. Over the last eighty-eight years, it has been occupied by four generations of the same family.

CONCLUSION

The disruption of World War I did not deter wealthy buyers from investing in the Wilson Island. Throughout the Roaring Twenties and the Great Depression, they were joined by speculators as well as families looking for a permanent home in the new upscale neighborhood. By 1940, 92 percent of the lots would host an eclectic display of period architectural styles designed by some of the notable architects of the era who took up residence in this part of town themselves. The families mentioned here are just a few examples of the people Rosanna Wilson envisioned living in the neighborhood.

When the very first buyers moved in, their homes were for the most part on a bare grid of empty dirt lots with views of the plains far to the north. Construction was initially slow and on some streets the entire side of a block laid vacant for a decade. The expanse of dirt was a daily reminder that this was the northern outer edge of residential life in Fresno at the time. But the wide open vacant lots provided an excellent playground for the neighborhood children. Early residents gradually saw families investing in their dream home begin construction alongside speculators hoping to profit from a quick turnover. Some occupied the homes they built. Others invested in homes they never intended to occupy but sold to business colleagues, who then resold them quickly. In several cases, multiple family members bought homes in the Wilson Island over a period of several generations. The first real deluge of buyers appeared in 1919 after the end of World War I.

Construction activity in and around the city in 1920 is an indication of how changes in Fresno contributed to their interest in the new neighborhood. Street improvements in 1920 suggest the vast plains to the north would soon host a network of motorways for the emerging automobile. Stretching from downtown up Blackstone and including side streets in neighborhoods near the Wilson Island, workers added sidewalks, curbs, cement gutters, and pavement. And it was Wilson Island resident Claude Thompson's company that won many of these contracts. Several other Wilson Islanders were active participants in the financing, design, and construction of commercial and residential buildings as well as industries with tentacles across the Central San Joaquin Valley.

Downtown was still the cultural center. That year, the proposed construction of a motion picture theatre was announced twice in the *Southwest Building and Contractor* (volume 55, pages 14 and 20). In January 1920, the

Kinema Investment Company announced the construction of a motion picture theatre at 1317-21 J Street (now Fulton) at a cost of $200,000. The San Francisco architect preparing the plans would ensure the building could accommodate a $50,000 organ for showing silent movies and seat three thousand. The structure would have double walls, concrete on the outside and adobe on the inside, and an air-cooling system. Adjacent to the structure along J Street would be shop spaces. Two months later, Alexander Pantages announced the construction of a theatre on L Street between Tulare and Kern (south of the Court House) for the "Pantages circuit," also at a cost of $200,000. Again, a San Francisco architect was drawing up the plans, this time to seat 3,750 and to include various furnishings valued at $100,000. Kinema and Pantages may have been referring to the same structure while looking for the best location. It is presumably what we know today as the Warnor Theatre at Tuolumne and Fulton, a block north of 1317-21 J Street, which still hosts the original pipe organ. It would not be until 1939 that the Tower Theatre would be built at Olive and Wishon across from the Wilsons' estate on the block where they had wanted A.G. Wishon to place his home.

What did the residents of this historic district have in common, and how were they different? They were the movers and shakers of the early 1900s in Fresno, some having descended from the city fathers and mothers of the late 1800s.[38] Husbands and wives alike were active contributors to Fresno's expanding community, all willing to make a personal commitment to northern residential expansion. They were frequently part of an extensive, established network through their membership in fraternal organizations, social clubs, sports, and civic interests. Their professions varied as widely as their tenure in Fresno—from new arrivals to Nob Hill sons and daughters.

To this day, the Wilson Island is a monument to the vision and determination of one person, Rosanna Cooper Wilson. The residents, then and now, have brought Rosanna's vision to life. Some stayed for decades while others followed the residential movement farther north to neighborhoods near Fresno High School on Echo Avenue, to nearby Fresno Normal School, and beyond to Fig Garden. Today, we owe a debt of gratitude to those whose foresight created a residential museum for the enjoyment of its twenty-first-century occupants. One hundred years later, their homes give us a glimpse of fashionable dwellings in the era when automobiles were first making an appearance and the notion of a suburb was just beginning to form.

POSTSCRIPT

AND TODAY?

The character of the Wilson Island, infused from its inception in the early 1900s, includes a strong sense of community that has survived for a century, passed on by generations of homeowners. The island is defined by something more than its snazzy, turn-of-the-twentieth-century homes. It is a village that values communication and social gatherings as much as a shared appreciation of Fresno's history. It's a place where homeowners know that maintaining their century-old homes also maintains a piece of the history of Fresno for future generations, to say nothing of their value. That shared responsibility makes the Wilson Island somewhat unique by today's suburban standards, and it began with the first residents.

In Rosanna's era, the women of the neighborhood came together in the Parlor Lecture Club, the Garden Club, the bridge and social clubs, while the men came together at Elks meetings and in business ventures. They all knew one another and shared an interest in developing Fresno. Today, the opportunities for connecting have changed, becoming more inclusive, but the outcome of a sense of belonging remains the same. Activities that now bring the diversity of residents together have a twenty-first-century flair. It's the newsletter and the email announcements that keep everyone informed. It's the sunflower-growing contest that begins each spring. It's the summer block party when we shut down a street, bring lawn chairs and food, chat, and listen to the neighborhood musicians until past sunset. It's the poetry readings and the annual potluck gathering of current and past residents at New Year's. It's the shared produce from backyard vegetable gardens, along with seeds and seedlings that erupt in a proliferation of Flanders poppies and oak trees. And it's the evening group of dog walkers who make the circuit on the Wilson Island streets signaling the end of the day. It's waving hello to the letter carrier who drops our mail in the old front door slots and knows our pets by name.

So, when does a neighborhood become a community? Perhaps it is when a shared sense of continuity as well as preservation takes precedence over change for change sake. Certainly the Tower District Specific Plan helped with its mention of this neighborhood as one worthy of special attention. But it took more than that. Well before the plan existed, for a hundred years a succession of homeowners ensured the sustainability of the neighborhood with the care they took to preserve their homes and with their interest in one another.

The homes in the Wilson Island rarely go on the market. It is not uncommon for ownership to remain in the same family for decades, handed down from one generation to the next. When they do turn over, word of mouth of a potential sale is way ahead of any realtor's posting. Longtime residents enthusiastically welcome young families with an eager hope that their children will be the next generation to continue the Wilson Island traditions and appreciate our eclectic differences.

Rosanna's role in creating the Wilson Island is a story to be remembered. It was fortuitous that this young, educated woman whose childhood was spent in the fertile California coastal valleys around Monterey Bay landed in the Central San Joaquin Valley when she did with an appetite to develop land. A descendant of Alta Californians who settled on vast ranchos in the 1700s and 1800s, she is an example of their children who went on to influence commerce, culture, and land development in other parts of the state. Perhaps it was not happenstance that on the last lots she hung onto, primarily along Echo Avenue, she watched the construction of Spanish Revival-style homes.

The three-story mansion and the lush grounds of the Wilson estate that had been the centerpiece of advertising the Wilson's North Fresno Tract and the center of activity on their vast ranch fell victim to the same urban development that both Rosanna and George promoted. Following her husband's death in 1915, she remained at the Wilson estate on the northeast block of Olive and Wishon for the next thirty-two years until she died in 1947. From her office on the first floor of her home, the petite woman who barely reached five feet tall had astutely managed over thirty years of change on the land she turned into a much-needed residential area for the growing city. After a fire in the third story severely damaged the home, it was torn down, and the remaining land at 831 Olive Avenue, once the lush estate of the landowner, was finally divided into lots that now host a variety of commercial enterprises. Rosanna never lived in the Wilson Island house her son built at 1445 Echo. Always a business woman, she regarded it as an investment to hang onto until the Depression ended though she kept it in the family for much longer. If we listen carefully, we may hear her softly signing us Spanish lullabies as she continues to watch over the neighborhood from her final resting place not far away at Mountain View Cemetery on Belmont Avenue.

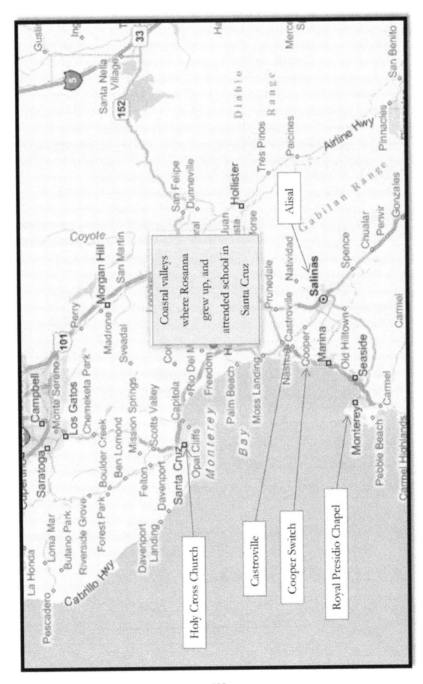

APPENDIX B
CALIFORNIA REGISTERED HISTORIC LANDMARKS
RELATED TO ROSANNA
(California Registered Historical Landmark number unless otherwise indicated)

HER COOPER GRANDFATHER'S HOME (MONTEREY COUNTY):

- **NATIONAL TRUST SITE: COOPER-MOLERA ADOBE, MONTEREY, CALIFORNIA**

  Cooper-Molera is significant as the original home of John Bautista Rogers Cooper, an American sea captain who settled in Monterey during Mexican rule in the early twentieth century. Cooper became a successful merchant and acquired extensive landholdings throughout Northern California. His wife, Encarnación Vallejo Cooper, was the sister of General Mariano Vallejo, who played an important role in California's transition from Mexican rule to an American territory. Subsequent generations of the Cooper family made significant contributions to the development of agriculture in the Salinas Valley. Cooper-Molera showcases residential life in early Monterey, when the small port city was the social, economic, and political hub of California in the era prior to the Gold Rush.

  Location: The site is a contributing resource within the Monterey Old Town National Historic Landmark District.

HER COOPER GRANDFATHER'S SAWMILL (SONOMA COUNTY):

- **NO. 835 COOPER'S SAWMILL**

  In 1834, Mariano G. Vallejo's brother-in-law, John B. R. Cooper, constructed California's first known power-operated commercial sawmill.

In addition to sawing redwood lumber, the mill and surrounding settlement served as a barrier to Russian encroachment from the west. Located on Mark West Creek, the water-powered mill was destroyed by flood in the winter of 1840–41.

Location: SW corner, intersection of Mirabel and River Roads (P.M. 174) near Mirabel Park, eight miles west of Santa Rosa.

HOMES OF HER VALLEJO GRANDUNCLES (SONOMA COUNTY):

• NO. 4 GENERAL M. G. VALLEJO HOME

The home of General Mariano Guadalupe Vallejo known as "Lachryma Montis" (Tears of the Mountain), was built in 1850. Its name was derived from the springs that now are the source of Sonoma's water supply. General Vallejo, born at Monterey on July 7, 1808, was commander of the northern Mexican frontier, founder of the Pueblo of Sonoma, and a member of the first Constitutional Convention of California.

Location: Vallejo Home, Sonoma State Historic Park, Spain at Third Street West, Sonoma.

• NO. 501 SALVADOR VALLEJO ADOBE

This was the home of Captain Salvador Vallejo, brother of General Mariano G. Vallejo, who founded Sonoma. The adobe was built by Indian labor between 1836 and 1846 and was occupied by Captain Vallejo and his family until the Bear Flag Party seized Sonoma on June 4, 1846. Cumberland College, a Presbyterian coeducational boarding school, was located here from 1858 to 1864.

Location: 421 First Street West, Sonoma.

Her Vallejo granduncle's vineyard (Sonoma County):

- ### NO. 739 VINEYARD AND WINERY
  ### (SAN FRANCISCO SOLANO MISSION VINEYARD)
  Here the Franciscan Fathers of San Francisco Solano de Sonoma Mission produced sacramental wine from the first vineyard in Sonoma Valley, planted in 1825. After secularization of the mission in 1835, General Mariano G. Vallejo, Commandant of Alta California's northern frontier, produced prize-winning wines from these grapes. A young immigrant from Italy, Samuele Sebastian, with his wife, Elvira, purchased this property in the early 1900s. Since that time, he and his family have continued with distinction the traditions handed down to them. Much of the original mission vineyard is still planted to choice wine grapes.

  Location: 394 Fourth Street East at Spain Street, Sonoma.

Her Vallejo great-grandfather's home (Monterey County):

- ### NO. 387 THE GLASS HOUSE,
  ### CASA MATERNA OF THE VALLEJOS
  In the 1820s, Don Ignacio Vallejo built the Casa Materna on Bolsa de San Cayetano. Don Ignacio and Dona Maria Antonio Lugo y Vallejo had thirteen children, eight daughters and five sons, one of whom was General Mariano Guadalupe Vallejo.

  Location: On edge of bluff one thousand feet north of intersection of Hillcrest Road and Salinas Road, 2.5 miles southeast of Watsonville.

HER BORONDA GRANDPARENTS FAMILY ADOBE (MONTEREY COUNTY):

- ### NO. 870 JOSÉ EUSEBIO BORONDA ADOBE CASA

  Built between 1844 and 1848 by José Eusebio Boronda, this is an outstanding example of a Mexican-era rancho adobe. Virtually unaltered since its construction, it shows many features of the "Monterey Colonial" style which resulted from the fusion of New England and California building traditions during California's Mexican period.
  Location: Salinas.

HER GRANDFATHER'S HALF-BROTHER (MONTEREY COUNTY):

- ### NO. 106 LARKIN HOUSE

  The adobe-and-wood Larkin House was built in 1835 by Thomas Oliver Larkin, a Yankee merchant who came to California in April 1832. Since Larkin was the only US consul to California under Mexican rule, his home became the American consulate from 1844 to 1846, and it was also used as military headquarters by Kearny, Mason, and Sherman.
  Location: Monterey State Historic Park, southwest corner of Jefferson and Calle Principal, Monterey.

- ### NO. 353 HOUSE OF FOUR WINDS

  In the late 1830s, Thomas Oliver Larkin built the House of Four Winds, named for the weather vane in his garden. Tradition says the building was used as an early hall of records.
  Location: 540 Calle Principal, Monterey.

APPENDIX C
PAJARO VALLEY CONSOLIDATED RAILROAD

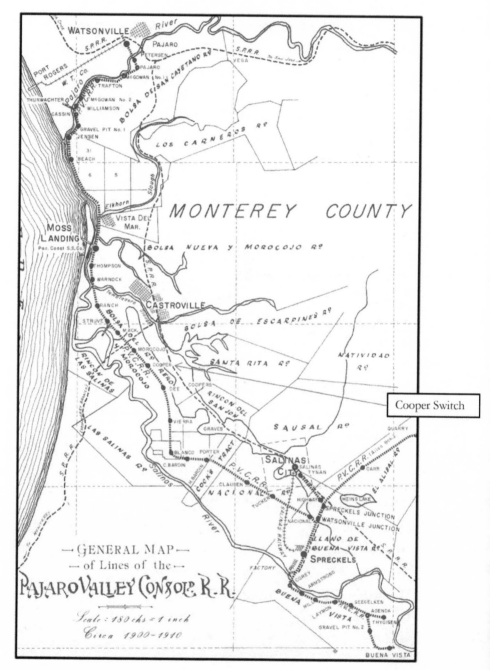

Cooper Switch

APPENDIX D
WILSON'S NORTH FRESNO TRACT MAP
Approved November 1908 (Rosanna's)

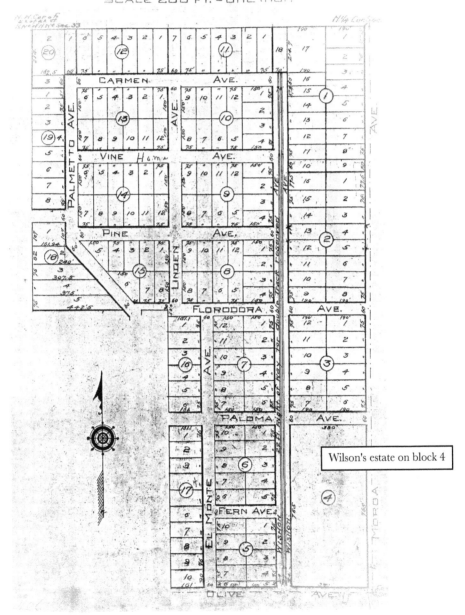

Wilson's estate on block 4

APPENDIX E
ALHAMBRA TRACT (DELFINA'S)
Filed 1910

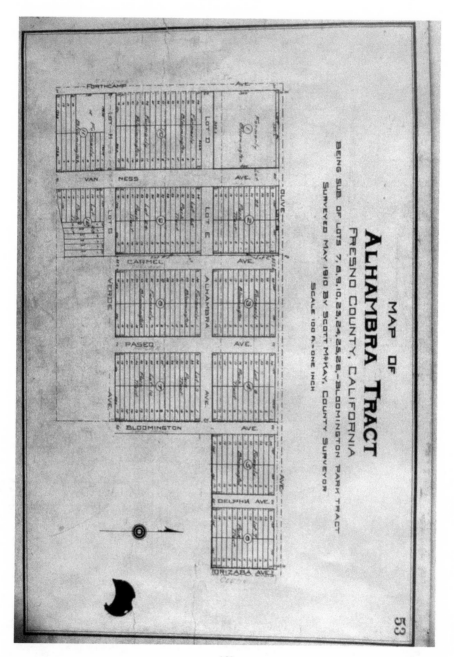

Appendix F
Streets in the Wilson Island that Changed Names

Wilson's North Fresno Tract (Rosanna)

1908 Street Name	2018 Street Name
Palmetto	Echo
Moroa	Maroa
El Monte (below Floradora)	Linden
Paloma	Hedges
Vine	Home
(not in original plan in block 4)	Fern

Alhambra Tract (Delfina)

1908 Street Name	2018 Street Name
Carmel	College
Paseo	Poplar
Bloomington (name of tract a portion of which was included in the Alhambra Tract)	San Pablo
Verde	Elizabeth
Alhambra	Alhambra
Orizaba	Glenn
Delphia	Delphia

APPENDIX G
ROSANNA'S MATERNAL AND PATERNAL ANCESTORS, CHILDREN AND GRANDCHILDREN

Rosanna's Maternal Ancestors

(tinted boxes are principal characters in the story)

The Borondas

Great-great-grandfather
Josef Manuel Boronda
(aka Jose Manuel Boronda)
1750–1826

Great-great-grandmother
Maria Gertrudis Higuera
1776–1851

The Sotos

Great great-grandfather
Ygnacio Soto
1748–1807

Great-great-grandmother
Maria Barbara Espinosa
1759–1797

Great-grandfather
Damaso Soto
1778–1827

Great-grandmother
Maria Antonia de Jesus Alviso
1795–unknown

Grandfather
Andres Soto
1813–1893

The Espinosas

Great-grandfather
Jose Gabriel Simon Espinosa
1791–1839

Great-grandmother
Maria Guadalupe Antonia Manerto Boronda
(aka Maria Guadalupe Marietta Boronda)
1801–after 1845

Grandmother
Maria Josefa Escolastica Espinosa
(aka Josefa Boronda)
1819–unknown

Father – JBHC
John Baptist Henry Cooper
(aka Henry Baptiste Guillermo Cooper)
1830–1899

Mother
Eduviguies (Ida) Soto
1839–1901

Rosanna Josefa Cooper
1859–1947

Husband
George Albert Wilson
1855–1915

Sister
Delfina Eduviguies Cooper
1862–1929

Sister
Guadalupe Cooper
1863–1890

Brother-in-law
James Page Long
1859–1935

Sister
Francisca Cooper
1866–1881

Rosanna's Paternal Ancestors, Children, and Grandchildren

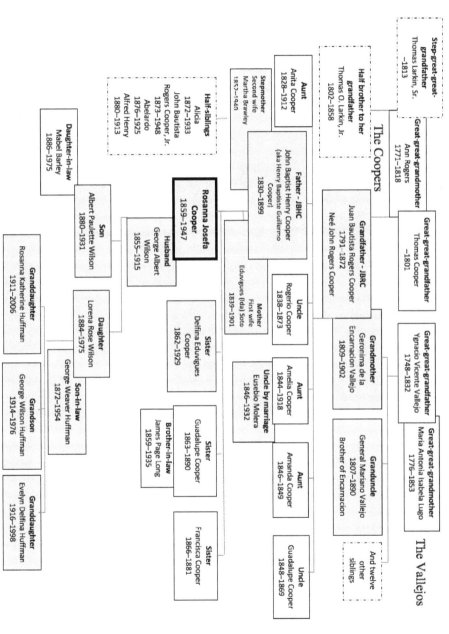

Step-great-great-grandfather
Thomas Larkin, Sr.
–1813

Half brother to her grandfather
Thomas O. Larkin, Jr.
1802–1858

Great-great-grandfather
Ann Rogers
1771–1818

Great-great-grandfather
Thomas Cooper
–1801

The Coopers

Aunt
Anita Cooper
1828–1912

Stepmother
Second wife
Martha Brawley
1817–1940

Half-siblings
Alicia 1872–1933
John Bautista Rogers Cooper, Jr. 1873–1948
Abelardo 1876–1925
Alfred Henry 1880–1913

Father - JBHC
John Baptist Henry Cooper
(aka Henry Baptiste Guillermo Cooper)
1830–1899

Grandfather - JBRC
Juan Bautista Rogers Cooper
1791–1872
Neé John Rogers Cooper

Grandmother
Geronima de la
Encarnación Vallejo
1809–1902

Daughter-in-law
Mabel Barley
1886–1975

Son
Albert Paulette Wilson
1880–1931

Rosanna Josefa Cooper
1859–1947

Husband
George Albert Wilson
1855–1915

Mother
First wife
Eduvigues (Ida) Soto
1839–1901

Uncle
Rogerio Cooper
1838–1873

Aunt
Amelia Cooper
1844–1918

Uncle by marriage
Eusebio Molera
1846–1932

Aunt
Amanda Cooper
1846–1849

The Vallejos

Great-great-grandfather
Ygnacio Vicente Vallejo
1748–1832

Great-great-grandmother
Maria Antonia Isabela Lugo
1776–1853

Granduncle
General Mariano Vallejo
1807–1890
Brother of Encarnación

And twelve other siblings

Uncle
Guadalupe Cooper
1848–1869

Granddaughter
Rosanna Katherine Huffman
1911–2006

Daughter
Lorena Rose Wilson
1884–1975

Sister
Delfina Eduvigues Cooper
1862–1929

Son-in-law
George Weaver Huffman
1872–1954

Sister
Guadalupe Cooper
1863–1890

Brother-in-law
James Page Long
1859–1935

Sister
Francisca Cooper
1866–1881

Grandson
George Wilson Huffman
1914–1976

Granddaughter
Evelyn Delfina Huffman
1916–1998

165

Endnotes

1   Source: Monterey Historical Society: http://mchsmuseum.com/borondaadobe.html.

2   These grants of land are known as Rancho Grants and were granted in order to encourage agriculture and industry, reward soldiers, and provide for settlers who held no property. These land grants were limited to a maximum size of eleven square leagues; most were smaller, and a few were larger. Source: Ranchos of California; UCB at: http://www.lib.berkeley.edu/libraries/earth-sciences-library

3   Additional information about how land grants were acquired is available at: http://www.lib.berkeley.edu/libraries/earth-sciences-library

4   The Boronda rancho was between Cooper's Rancho Bolsa del Potrero y Moro Cojo on the west, Castro's Rancho Sausal on the east, and Espinosa's Rancho Bolsa de las Escorpinas on the north. The grant was on the northwest of present-day Salinas. Today the adobe is California Historic Landmark No. 870.

5   General Vallejo was born at Monterey July 7, 1808, and spent his final years at his home built in 1850, known as "Lachryma Montis" (Tears of the Mountain) near Sonoma. Its name was derived from the springs

that are now the source of Sonoma's water supply. His home is registered California Landmark No. 4.

6 "He proposed to deed to the state 156 acres of land bordering the Straits of Carquinez, and to donate the sum of $360,000 for the erection and furnishing or equipping of the state capitol, governor's mansion, and other state buildings, a state university, library, state botanical gardens, asylums, penitentiary, hospitals and orphanage" (McKittrick 1944). The legislature met in Vallejo for the first time in 1851 but was subsequently moved to Sacramento due to lack of sufficient progress on building construction and political pressure.

7 In 1834, Juan B. R. Cooper constructed California's first known power-operated commercial sawmill. In addition to sawing redwood lumber, the mill and surrounding settlement served as a barrier to Russian encroachment from the west. Located on Mark West Creek, the water-powered mill was destroyed by flood in the winter of 1840–41. Registered California Landmark No. 835.

8 Andres Soto married Maria Josefa Escolastica Espinosa on October 6, 1834. However, the baptismal record for his daughter Eduvigues Soto on October 29, 1839, states her mother was Josefa Boronda. This is the same person. The priest entering Josefa's family name on Eduvigues's baptismal record used her mother's maiden name, Boronda, instead of her married name, Espinosa, not uncommon at the time.

9 A vestige of Alisal today is the street by that name in downtown Salinas.

10 Source: 1870 census for Castroville and San Francisco.

11 Source: *Cooper* by John Woolfenden and Amelie Elkinton, 1983, p. 102.

12 Source: Clovis, p. 17.

13 For many years, Eduvigues was known by her nickname, Ida. Variations in spelling used by federal census enumerators attest to the challenges in identifying the spelling that best captures the pronunciation of her given name. "Eduvigues" will be used in the remainder of this manuscript.

14 Cathedral San Carlos Borromeo, or the Royal Presidio Chapel, is California Historic Landmark No. 135.

15 The county was a desert, "fit only for pasturage and worthless for agriculture . . . lacking the water to make it productive." The immense tule swamps " . . . were visited by the Spaniards and the Californians in pursuit of deserting Indians, and horse and cattle thieves" (Vandor 1919).

16 Source: Wilson v. Cooper appeal, 1932.

17 Millions had been loaned by outside banks in San Francisco and Sacramento at valuations based on speculative terms. The whole Central Valley was affected (Winchell 1933).

18 This may have been a reference to a tire or tire pump. He reminds his father with every letter how important it is and tells him that it is the latest improvement for bicycles.

19 This is now the address for the Chicken Pie Shop in the Tower District.

20 For its first forty years, Fulton was called Forthcamp, named for early Fresno resident J. D. Forthcamp, a foreman for early land promoter August Weihe. The name Forthcamp continued north from Divisidero for one mile to Olive Avenue, "where the conditions of land ownership

called for a jog westward of 100 feet on Olive before the northward routing continued" (Walker 1941). The condition referred to is the block owned by George and Rosanna on which they built their three-story home. In 1939, the electric car rails were removed from Fulton to enhance traffic flow from downtown. That same year, the Tower Theatre was built.

21 Their address was 831 Olive Avenue. Today, this block is bordered on the south by Olive Avenue, on the north by Fern Street, on the west by Wishon Avenue, and on the east by Maroa Avenue. The block houses the Chicken Pie Shop and Roger Rocka's.

22 Rosanna filed the tract map with the city in November 1908 for a residential development that extended from Olive to McKinley, and from Echo to Maroa (initially spelled Moroa).

23 Source: Original 1909 contract.

24 Per the original document: The agreement was for " . . . cows, heifers and increase thereof [to be] reared, tamed, and milked, and in all things used as dairy cows." He required " . . . pay for any cows, heifers, or calf that may die through neglect the market value of said animals." And he " . . . agreed to furnish. . . three good saddle horses and one mule with pack saddle and equipments [sic], to be returned to [him] at the termination hereof."

25 Their office was located at 317 Pacific Avenue, Santa Cruz, California.

26 Martha's second marriage in 1904 was to Pedro (Peter) Vasquez, one of her ranch hands at the El Sur Ranch. Peter was a descendent of one of the most prominent families to come from Mexico to settle in

Monterey County. However, he was also the nephew of the notorious Monterey bandit, Tiburcio Vasquez, who was hanged in San Jose in 1875. The marriage only lasted until 1909 when she divorced him (Monterey State Historic Association 2014).

27 The Cooper-Molera Adobe was still under renovation as of January 2018.

28 For a more complete history of Fresno High School, refer to the article by John Walker in *Historical Perspectives*, "The Original Fresno High School," May 16, 2011. Available at the main Fresno library.

29 Although the language used in the original deeds alludes to horses as a necessary form of transportation, an indication of the socioeconomic level of the early buyers is the number of building permits issued to them and/or their contractors for both a house and a garage. It was not until the late 1920s that the automobile became popular with the general public, bringing with it the need for a garage. Among the Wilson Island residents who built homes between 1919 and 1921, at least twelve building permits, virtually half of them, were obtained for a house with a garage.

30 Paloma became Hedges. For a list of street name changes, see Appendix F.

31 The buyers were Charles T. and Rhoda J. Cearly (stationary store owners and publisher of the Fresno City Directories), who purchased and moved to a second home in the Wilson Island in 1926 at 624 Pine.

32 1525 N Echo, 1487 N Echo, 1445 N Echo, 625 E Home, 667 E Home, 601 E Pine, and 640 E. Pine.

33 In the original tract map, only seven lots were not 75 feet by 150 feet. These were in blocks 15 and 18 at the intersection of Echo and

Floradora, configured differently than it appears today. In the course of selling her lots, Rosanna allowed about a dozen buyers to purchase larger lots. Today, there are eighty homes in the Wilson Island, seventy-eight of which are considered historic properties.

34 The third lot was at 605 Carmen, also purchased with Frank Petty in 1919. They sold it the same year to Fresno Planing Mill owner C. W. Bingham, who had the house built.

35 According to Ben Walker, "In the 1880s, K Street [now Van Ness Avenue] between Tulare and Kern was 'Nob Hill,' with what were then the mansions of Louis Einstein and Louis Gundelfinger on the westerly side and the smaller cottages of Dr. Chester Rowell . . . and others. In the block further south, between Kern and Inyo, there were the larger houses of Herman Levy, the clothier and father of the four Levy Brothers, insurance and realty men today, F. D. Vanderlip, Leopold Gundelfinger . . ." (1941). The residences of the Einsteins and Gundelfingers (who are related by marriage) were the most prestigious of their day. By 1917, they were removed to make way for city expansion (Vandor 1919).

36 Additional information about the Fresno Brewing Company and William Eilert is provided in the article by John Walker in *Historical Perspectives*, in November 7, 2010: "Fresno Brewing Company" available at the Main Fresno Library.

37 Roual Deacon owned Lemoore Lumber Company. After purchasing the lot and constructing the house on Carmen, he lived in the home for about two years before turning it over to Eilert and moving north to the corner of Maroa and Yale Avenues in the new home built for him by Swartz and Ryland. Within the same period, these architects

had also designed the A. B. Knapp home at 708 Carmen and the Ben Kauffman residence at 708 Home Avenue.

38 In July 1885, 121 of Fresno's businessmen signed the petition to incorporate the City of Fresno. They included five men whose sons or nephews built homes in the Wilson Island: Louis Einstein, Herman Levy, W. F. Rowe, and Chester Rowell. George Wilson's brother, F. B. Wilson, also signed the petition. George and Rosanna would not arrive in Fresno until the following year.

BIBLIOGRAPHY

Primary and Secondary Resources:

Anderson, Burton. *A Native Son's History of the Central Coast*. Monterey County, CA: Monterey County Historical Society Publication, 2010.

Anderson, Burton. *From Valley to Sea, 25 Years with the Coastal Grower*. Monterey County, CA: Monterey County Historical Society Publication, 2015.

Barrows, Henry. *Memorial and Biographical History of the Coast Counties of Central California*. Chicago, Lewis Publishing Company, 1893.

Clark, Donald Thomas. *Monterey County Place Names, a Geographical Dictionary*. University Librarian Emeritus. UC, Santa Cruz, Kestral Press, Carmel Valley, California, 1991.

Clark Historic Research Consultants. "Agriculturally Related Historic Resources Located in the Unincorporated Areas Between Salinas and Soledad, Monterey County, California." Prepared for Monterey County Historic Resources Review Board, Monterey County Parks Department, Salinas, California, September 2000.

Clovis, Margaret. *Images of America, Monterey County's North Coast and Coastal Valleys*. Charleston, SC: Arcadia Publishing, 2006.

Cowan, Robert G. *Ranchos of California: a list of Spanish Concessions 1775–1822 and Mexican Land Grants 1822–1846*. Fresno, CA: Academy Library Guild, 1956.

Davis, Ellis A. *Davis's Commercial Encyclopedia of the Pacific Southwest*. Oakland, 1915.

Ewing, McDaniel and Meux, Inc. "City of Fresno and Additions," Map, 1915.

"Fresno Home Is Sold for $23,000." *The Fresno Bee*. December 26, 1924, page 1.

"Great Demand for More Houses in Fresno City." *The Fresno Morning Republican*, January 5, 1908, page 4.

Guinn, J. M. *History of the State of California and Biographical Record of the San Joaquin Valley, California*. Chicago: The Chapman Publishing Company, 1905.

Harrison, Edward S. *History of Santa Cruz County, California*. San Francisco: Pacific Press Publishing Company, 1892.

Hattersley-Drayton, Karana, and Jeannine Raymond. "Historic Property Survey Report and Local Historic District Nomination for the Wilson Island, Fresno, California." September 8, 2009.

Koch, Margaret. *Santa Cruz County, Parade of the Past*. Fresno, CA: Valley Publishers, 1973.

Larkin, Thomas O. *The Larkin Papers for the History of California*. Volume II, 1843–1844. George P. Hammond, editor. Berkeley, CA: University of California Press, 1952.

Martin, Dan R. "Bull-bear Fights Thrilled Crowds." Monterey County History of Salinas Index. July 1821, 1940.

Martin, Edward. *History of Santa Cruz County, California with Biographical Sketches*. Los Angeles: Historic Record Company, 1911.

McAlester, Virgina and Lee. *A Field Guide to America's Historic Neighborhoods and Museum Houses; The Western States*. New York: Alfred A. Knopf, 1998.

McKittrick, Myrtle M. *Vallejo, Son of California*. Portland, OR: Binfords & Mort Publishers, 1944.

Merritt, Joseph. "Resources and Property of Castroville, Sketch of the Town and Vicinity." In *History of Monterey County*. San Francisco: Elliott and Moore Publishers, 1881.

Monterey State Historic Park Association. "Strong-willed Martha Brawley's Rise to Wealth and Social Prominence." July–September 2014, pp. 4–6.

Monterey County Directory: Listing of All Adult Residents in the Townships in Monterey County. Salt Lake City: Family History Library, 1889.

Rosenus, Alan. *General Vallejo and the Advent of the Americans.* Berkeley, CA: Heyday Books/Urion Press, 1999.

Salinas Californian. "These People Settled the Boronda district." June 22,1968.

Street and Road Map of Fresno, California. Bekins Van & Storage, 1926.

"Tower District Specific Plan," City of Fresno, Development Department, Planning Division; Wallace Roberts and Todd; Robert Bruce Anderson; March 26, 1991.

Vandor, Paul E. *The History of Fresno County, California with Biographical Sketches.* Los Angeles: Historic Record Company, 1919.

Walker, Ben R., editor-in-chief. *Fresno Community Book.* Arthur H. Cawston, Managing Editor and Publisher, 1946.

Walker, Ben R. *The Fresno County Blue Book.* Arthur H. Cawston, Editor and Publisher, 1941.

Walker, Ben R. Clipping files maintained by the Fresno City and County Historical Society.

Wall, Rosalind Sharpe. *A Wild Coast and Lonely; Big Sur Pioneers.* San Carlos, CA: Wild World Publishing/Tetra, 1989.

Western Union Telegraph Company. *Journal of the Telegraph: A Record of the Progress of the Telegraph and Electrical Science.* Volume XV. New York: W. F. Vanden Houten, 1882.

Wilson v. Cooper. Court of Appeal of California. First District, Division Two.126 Cal. App. 607 (Cal. Ct. App. 1932).

Winchell, Ernestine. "Olive, At North Fulton." *Fresno Republican.* October 13, 1929, page 4.

Winchell, Lilbourne Alsip. *History of Fresno County and the San Joaquin Valley*. Ben Walker, editor. Fresno, CA: A. H. Cawston, 1933.

Woolfenden, John, and Elkinton, Amelie. *Cooper, Juan Bautista Rogers Cooper*. Pacific Grove, CA: The Boxwood Press, 1983.

Online Resources

Heath, Earl, editor. 2014. "Seventy-Five Years of Progress: An Historical Sketch of the Southern Pacific, 1869–1944." *Central Pacific Railroad Photographic History Museum*. http://www.cprr.org/Museum/SP_1869-1944/.

McDonald, Douglas Shaver. 2012. "C.B. Shaver." *Central Sierra Historical Society*, March 5. http://www.sierrahistorical.org/c-b-shaver/.

Ormsby, Cameron. 2010. "Land Speculation in Fresno County: 1860–1891." *Stanford University Spatial History Lab*, September 1. https://web.stanford.edu/group/spatialhistory/media/images/publication/fresno_county_land_holders3.pdf.

Perez, Chris. 1982. "Ranchos of California." August 23. http://www.lib.berkeley.edu/EART/rancho.html.

Powell, John Edward. 1996. "Harrison B. Traver." *A Guide to Historic Architecture in Fresno, California*. http://historicfresno.org/bio/traver.htm.

"The Mining Boom: 1879–1893." *Aspen Historical Society*. http://aspenhistory.org/aspen-history/the-mining-boom-1879-1893/.

Southwest Builder and Contractor. 1920. Volume 55. Google Books. https://books.google.com/books/about/Southwest_Builder_and_Contractor.html?id=ko09AQAAMAAJ.

Walker, John. 2011. "Southern Pacific Depot." *Historical Perspectives*, August 20. https://www.fresnobee.com/news/special-reports/article19506027.html.

Walker, John. 2010. "Fresno Brewing Company." *Historical Perspectives*, November 7. No longer posted. Available at the Main Fresno Library.

Walker, John. 2010. "Fresno Street Cars." May 17. https://www.fresnobee.com/news/special-reports/article19505043.html.

Walker, John. 2011. "The Original Fresno High School." *Historical Perspectives,* May 16. https://www.fresnobee.com/news/special-reports/ article19510950.html.

Whaley, Derek R. 2018. "Stations: Ranch." *Santa Cruz Trains.* http://www. santacruztrains.com/2017/05/stations-ranch.html.

Note: Web links change over time as authors move their material to updated sites. For example, the John Walker Fresno Beehive materials were on a server that crashed and now the full articles are available only at the Main Fresno Library.

Interviews, Documents, and/or Photos Provided By:

Descendants of Rosanna Cooper Wilson, in particular:
> *Rosanna Katherine Huffman,* granddaughter of George A. and Rosanna C. Wilson, provided first-hand and anecdotal information about her grandparents, and access to documents.
> *Betsy Huffman Griffin,* great-granddaughter of George A. and Rosanna C. Wilson, provided anecdotal information and granted access to her family's private collection of voluminous documents, photos, and memorabilia.
> *Virginia Huffman Lipari,* great-granddaughter of George A. and Rosanna C. Wilson, shared copies of photos of the interior and exterior of the Wilson home at 831 East Olive Avenue.

Descendant of Guadalupe Cooper (Rosanna's sister and third daughter of Eduvigues Soto):
> Phil Long shared his research on original birth, baptismal, marriage, and death records.

Descendants of Wilson Island residents:
> *Robert Boro,* grandson of Herbert Levy (666 Home), supplied information about the neighborhood he grew up in.
> *The late William F. Mosgrove,* son of first homeowners, William A. and Nellie Mosgrove (660 Pine Avenue) provided information about initial owners and builders, including his father. W. F. Mosgrove was a real estate agent with considerable knowledge of the properties and owners in the Wilson Island.

Historians

> *John E. Powell* supplied information on specific homes and provided informal guidance in the discussions about how to define the Wilson Island during the preparation of the proposal for an historic district in 2009.
>
> *Roger B. Taylor*, local architectural historian, supplied information about Richard Felchlin.

Note: The history of ownership for each home was obtained from public documents available in the Fresno Hall of Records and the City Planning Office. Where dates of construction are estimated due to an absence of an initial building permit, the estimate is based on information from subsequent building permits, Sanborn maps, newspaper articles, and information from interviews with people familiar with the history of their home passed on by previous homeowners.

INDEX

About the Author

Jeannine Raymond is a native Californian who has traveled enough in the Far East, Europe, and the US over the last thirty years—in the third world as well as cosmopolitan centers—to know that Fresno is a comparatively decent place to live, undeserving of the many Fresno jokes it receives. She is also a Wilson Islander.

Life experiences build on each other. A forty year career in higher education culminating with a decade at the greatest university in the world, UC Berkeley (condolences to the Cardinal enclave down the road), honed skills now needed for the next 40 years. In 2017, she left academe to begin researching and writing non-fiction histories (an oxymoron?) of Fresno. The Wilson Island project is the epicenter.

When she is not buried in archives or writing stories, she is in one of her other spaces for creative expression, her garden or her beading. She is a certified University of California Master Gardener who likes to experiment, design, and work with nature in the many microclimates of the half acre she tends. And when the heat is too extreme to be outside, she may be working on the latest seed bead creation or visiting friends.

CPSIA information can be obtained
at www.ICGtesting.com
Printed in the USA
FSHW021253030419
56930FS